Classical Karaoke

for

Kids

by Marjorie Kiel Persons

including

LYRICS FOR CLASSICAL MUSIC

by Marjorie Kiel Persons

ILLUSTRATIONS

by Philip Nellis

PORTRAITS

by George Ann Johnson

A publication of
Marjorie & Clyde Persons
d/b/a CLASSICAL MAGIC®
PO Box 1809
Banner Elk, NC 28604-1809 USA

Copyright © 2003 CLASSICAL MAGIC®
PO Box 1809
Banner Elk, NC 28604

All rights reserved. Except as permitted under Copyright Law, no part of this publication including artwork may be reproduced, stored in a retrieval system, or transmitted by any means, electronic, mechanical, photocopying, recording or otherwise, without prior written permission of the copyright owner.

All lyrics © 1998, 2000, 2003 Marjorie Kiel Persons. All rights reserved.

Parents and teachers should use their own discretion to determine the suitability of certain lyrics for their children. Children should be supervised in the learning process. Neither the author nor Classical Magic shall have any liability nor responsibility for any inappropriate use of the contents of this book.

Visit the publishers web site at http://www.classicalmagic.net

International Standard Book Number: 0-9675997-2-5

Library of Congress Control Number: 2002114517

First Printing: January 2003

Publisher
Marjorie & Clyde Persons d/b/a CLASSICAL MAGIC®

Cover and Book Design and Layout
Marjorie & Clyde Persons

Composer Portraits
George Ann Johnson

Illustrator
Philip Nellis

CD Recording Studio
The Loft Studio, Boone, NC

Announcer
Tim Greene

Recording Engineer
Jim Price

Vocalists
Robert Matthews
Loree Hodge
Amy Young
Eddie Adams
Alex DeVine
Jessalyn DeVine

Keyboards
Robert Matthews
Alex DeVine

Violins
Seth Parker
Robin Parker

Trumpet
Brent Bingham

About the Author

Marjorie Persons is a *summa cum laude* graduate of Macalester College in St. Paul, Minnesota. She later completed post-graduate studies at the University of Minnesota and Kean College in Union, New Jersey. She is an experienced teacher with majors in Elementary, Secondary, Music, and Religious Education, as well as English Literature. She and her husband Clyde, an engineer, have lived in Venezuela, Aruba, Egypt and Mexico in addition to several regions of the United States. They currently live in the Blue Ridge Mountains of northwestern North Carolina.

Photo by Todd Bush

About the Illustrator

Philip Nellis has been drawing for as long as he can remember. His drawing during Mrs. Persons' literature classes in Oaxaca, Mexico, called her attention to his talent. She is pleased to feature his delightful illustrations in **Classical Magic's *Classical Karaoke for Kids***. Philip's parents and grandparents are missionaries in Oaxaca, Mexico. Philip and his wife, Ruth, live in Chicago where he is doing post-graduate work at Moody Bible Institute.

About the Portrait Artist

A native of Oklahoma, George Ann Johnson has been an active artist for over twenty years. Having a strong natural talent, she has studied at the Danforth Museum of Fine Art and with numerous nationally and internationally recognized artists. She has received numerous awards for her wildlife art and other fine art works. Her diverse talent is expressed in pencil and watercolor portraits, oil paintings, sculpture, etched glass, stained glass, flower arrangements, and one-of-a-kind fountains. She operates GAJ Studio in Narrows, Virginia, and Fountains & More Gallery in Peterstown, West Virginia.

About the Recording Engineer

Jim Price has been a freelance recording engineer for 14 years. He is a graduate of the Recording Engineering program at the Full Sail Center for the Recording Arts in Orlando, Fla. Since then he has worked in many of the studios in the Western North Carolina and Eastern Tennessee area, recording music of all styles. He has engineered several number-one and top-ten singles in Southern Gospel music, and recorded the Grammy Award-nominated album "Doc & Richard Watson - Third Generation Blues." Jim resides in Bristol, Tennessee with his wife Debbie.

Acknowledgments

Special thanks to:
    Appalachian State University Music Library and Music Education Department;
    Avery County Elementary Schools where Classical Magic® continues to flourish.

Thanks also to:
    Carol Cantrell, Larene DeVine, Teresa Ehrlich, Dudley Gilmer, Louise Kiel, Ellen Stapleton, and Joy Tuggy for proofreading;
    Tim Green, Jim Price and Sharon Yates of The Loft Recording Studio;
    and Clyde Persons, my husband, who spent many hours as project and business manager, bookkeeper, computer specialist, editor, encourager, and partner in **Classical Magic's** production of *Classical Karaoke for Kids.*

About the Vocalists (on the CD)

Robert Matthews, Loree Hodge, Amy Young, and Eddie Adams

Robert Matthews, our tenor, keyboard player and musical director, is originally from Pinehurst, North Carolina. After graduating from Appalachian State University with a degree in Music Education and Piano Performance, he is now teaching choral music at North Wilkes High School in Hays, North Carolina, where he was chosen "Teacher of the Year" for 2002 - 2003. In addition to teaching, Robert is currently working on a master's degree in choral conducting.

Loree James Hodge, our alto, is from Lenoir, North Carolina, where she teaches chorus and general music and gives private music lessons. She was selected "Teacher of the Year for 2001 - 2002. She received her Music Education Degree from Appalachian State University in Boone, North Carolina.

Amy Marie Young, our soprano, is from Catawba, North Carolina. As a student of Dr. Julia Pedigo, she received a degree in Vocal Performance from Appalachian State University. Amy is now working on her master's degree in Vocal Performance. While she will pursue a performance career, her dream is to open a business with performing opportunities for young talent.

Eddie Adams, our bass, is from Snow Hill, North Carolina. He is a Music Education major at Appalachian State University. Eddie studies voice under Dr. Joseph Amaya. Upon graduation he plans to attend graduate school. He believes that music plays a crucial role in a child's education.

Dedication

To my husband

Clyde Orval Persons

who has been and is the
Support System

for our adventure with

Classical Magic®

Books by Marjorie Kiel Persons

Themes To Remember, Volume 1
Themes To Remember, Volume 2
Teacher's Guide for Themes To Remember, Volume 1
Classical Karaoke for Kids

Foreword

Music is magical, and classical music is especially so. Recent studies show that it enhances learning and boosts our intellect. We hear it even before we are born; we are just beginning to realize how important classical music is for the child's brain development. We know that it inspires us, soothes us, and nourishes our soul. Can you imagine a world without music?

Maybe you have wanted to listen to classical music but didn't know where to begin. Would you like to be able to tell Bach from Haydn and to recognize some of their most famous music? **Classical Magic**® can help you recognize themes from classical music and be able to recall the names of both composer and composition in a very short time. And it's fun!

Classical Magic® is a **theme recognition** program based on lyrics by the author. These lyrics for classical music themes contain the names of both the composer and the composition. You'll be amazed at how quickly you begin to hear the themes you've learned. You may recognize them on TV or radio ads, on your cell phone or computer, in cartoons and movies, or in restaurants and elevators.

Children love **Classical Karaoke for Kids** because they can sing along with the best music mankind has composed. The abstract is made concrete for them. They interact with the music, learn it, and remember it. **Classical Karaoke for Kids** inspires children to listen to classical music, to play it on an instrument, and most of all, to enjoy it.

The **Classical Magic**® **Method** has been successfully tested with children from pre-school (ages 2 to 4) through high school. Their resulting love for, and recognition of, classical music has been truly amazing. Children will never outgrow classical music. **Early theme recognition sets the foundation for a lifetime adventure with classical music**.

Let **Classical Magic**® do its magic. Learn the themes quickly to build excitement. You'll enjoy it, and your children will be convinced that they are child prodigies!

How to Use CLASSICAL KARAOKE For KIDS

Bring out the microphones (real or pretend) and let the fun begin! Children love to sing lyrics along with the most beautiful themes of classical music. The lyrics contain the names of both composer and composition, and, like magic, the children learn both very quickly. When children recognize themes, they will enjoy listening to longer recorded selections.

Play "Name That Classical Theme"
The CD included with *Classical Karaoke for Kids* has two tracks for each of the 37 themes. The first odd-numbered track is music-only, and the second even-numbered track has the music with the lyrics for the **Karaoke Sing Along**. The "music-only" track is perfect for "**Name That Classical Theme**." Transparency masters are available so the words and illustrations can be projected for all to see. Sing as a class or have children sing duets, trios, quartets or solos. They'll beg you for more! (For 80 additional themes, see *Themes To Remember,* **Volumes 1 & 2**.)

Other Games

- **Name the Composer**
  Point to the picture of a composer. (Enlarged portraits are available.) A child may be asked to tell the composer's name and/or the name of one of his compositions.
- **Who Am I?**
  A child pretends to be a composer and gives progressively more clues until someone guesses his identity.
- **Hum a Theme**
  A child hums a theme for others to guess. Use a microphone for this.

Classroom Teachers
Classical Karaoke for Kids is designed for use by classroom teachers as well as music teachers. You need no previous musical training to use it effectively. It takes very little time to introduce a new theme each week and sing the theme every day for that week. Most themes take less than a minute to sing. **Classical Magic**® works wonders in those "empty" spaces when children arrive in the morning or when getting ready to change classes. The music can also be played during art, free reading time, or project time. It can be used as a reward for hard work or good behavior. Once children learn a few themes, they'll want to learn more than one new theme a week.

Meet the Composers
Composers are listed by historical period. Older children can start to understand that music, literature, and art reflect the period in which they were produced. They will enjoy reading about the composers and relating them to historical and cultural events.

Piano and Forte
Piano, a quiet little cat, and **Forte**, a rather loud little dog, will accompany you throughout the book. **Allegro**, the speedy little mouse, also sneaks into some of the illustrations! You will find a reproducible pattern for puppets on page ix. Enlarge them, if you wish. Let Piano sing the quiet parts of a theme, and Forte can sing the loud portions.

Movement
Children love to pretend. Be conductors, play the violin or the timpani, stomp grapes with Bach, march with the *Turks*, and act out the *Clock* Symphony. Let children use their imaginations. Keep a sense of humor and a light-hearted attitude. Children learn when they are having fun!

Patterns for Stick Puppets--Piano, Forte, and Allegro

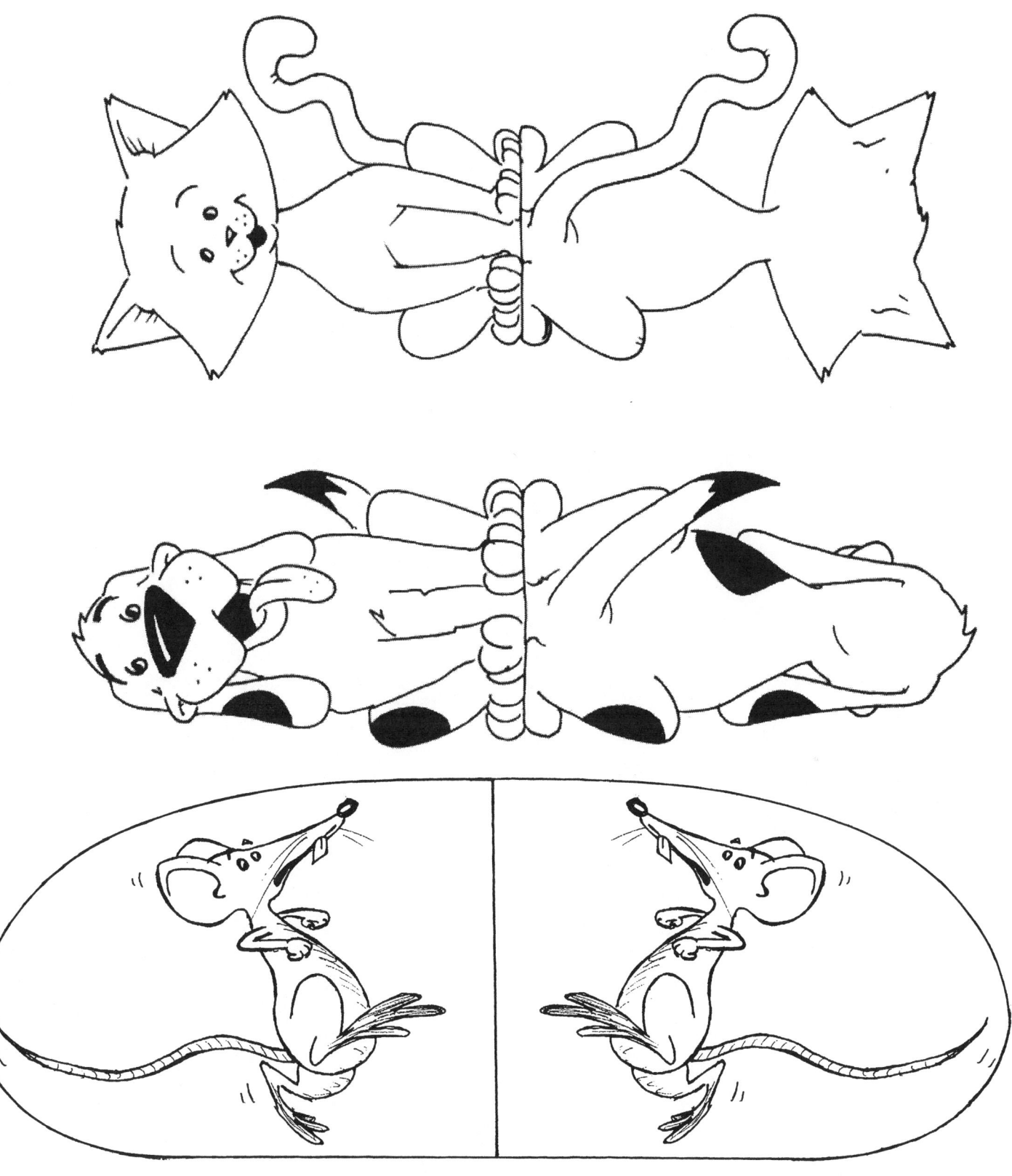

For best results, enlarge the images.
Copyright 2003 by Classical Magic® - **Reproducible for classroom teaching only.** All other rights reserved.

ix

Classical Karaoke for Kids

BAROQUE

Pachelbel
Bach
Scarlatti
Handel

CLASSICAL

Haydn
Mozart
Beethoven
Schubert

ROMANTIC

Mendelssohn	Smetana
Chopin	Strauss
Wagner	Brahms
Verdi	Ponchielli
Offenbach	Tchaikovsky

MODERN

Debussy
Satie
Joplin
Stravinsky
Prokofiev

Table of Contents

Foreword — vii

How to use CLASSICAL MAGIC's *Classical Karaoke for Kids* — viii

Piano, Forte, and Allegro Puppet Patterns — ix

TIMELINE OF COMPOSERS — 2

THE BAROQUE PERIOD (c. 1600 - 1750) — 5

<u>CD Tracks</u>

PACHELBEL, Johann — 6
    Canon in D — [1] & [2] — 7

BACH, Johann Sebastian — 8
    Orchestral Suite No.1, Bourée II — [3] & [4] — 9
    Minuet in G — [5] & [6] — 10
    Orchestral Suite No.1, Courante — [7] & [8] — 12

SCARLATTI, Domenico — 14
    Sonata in E, K. 38 — [9] & [10] — 15

HANDEL, George Frideric — 16
    The Harmonious Blacksmith — [11] & [12] — 17

Questions for the Musical Prodigy - Baroque Period — 18

Good Listening from the Baroque Period — 19

Contents

THE CLASSICAL PERIOD   (1750 - 1820)   21

	CD Tracks	
Musical Forms of the Classical Period		22
Symphony Orchestra Seating Plan		23
HAYDN, Franz Joseph		24
The *Clock* Symphony 101, Mvt. 1	[13] & [14]	25
The *Clock* Symphony 101, Mvt. 2	[15] & [16]	27
The *Clock* Symphony 101, Mvt. 3	[17] & [18]	32
The *Clock* Symphony 101, Mvt. 4	[19] & [20]	33
Drum Roll Symphony 103, Mvt. 4	[21] & [22]	34
MOZART, Wolfgang Amadeus		36
Minuet from *Don Juan*	[23] & [24]	37
Piano Sonata in C, K. 545	[25] & [26]	37
BEETHOVEN, Ludwig van		38
Für Elise	[27] & [28]	39
Turkish March from *The Ruins of Athens*	[29] & [30]	40
Symphony No. 5, Mvt. 4	[31] & [32]	41
SCHUBERT, Franz		42
Serenade	[33] & [34]	43
Questions for the Musical Prodigy - Classical Period		44
Good Listening from the Classical Period		45

Contents

THE ROMANTIC PERIOD (1820 - 1900) — 47

	CD Tracks	
MENDELSSOHN, Felix		48
Spring Song	[35] & [36]	49
CHOPIN, Frédéric		50
Fantasie-Impromptu	[37] & [38]	51
Tristesse Etude	[39] & [40]	52
WAGNER, Richard		54
Ride of the Valkyries	[41] & [42]	55
VERDI, Giuseppe		56
Nabucco - Story of the Opera		57
Nabucco - Chorus of Hebrew Slaves	[43] & [44]	59
Aïda - Story of the Opera		60
Triumphal March from *Aïda*	[45] & [46]	61
OFFENBACH, Jacques		62
Can Can from *Orpheus in the Underworld*	[47] & [48]	63
The Greek Myth of *Orpheus and Eurydice*		64
Orpheus in the Underworld	[49] & [50]	65
SMETANA, Bedřich		66
The Moldau from *My Country*	[51] & [52]	67
STRAUSS, Johann		68
Waltz from *Die Fledermaus*	[53[& [54]	69
BRAHMS, Johannes		70
Symphony No. 1, Mvt. 4	[55] & [56]	71
PONCHIELLI, Almicare		72
Dance of the Hours - from *La Gioconda*	[57] & [58]	73
TCHAIKOVSKY, Peter Ilyich		74
Piano Concerto No. 1 in B♭ minor, Mvt. 1	[59] & [60]	75
The Story of *Sleeping Beauty*		76
Sleeping Beauty	[61] & [62]	77
Shakespeare's *Romeo and Juliet*		78
Romeo and Juliet	[63] & [64]	79

Questions for the Musical Prodigy - Romantic Period — 80

Good Listening from the Romantic Period — 81

Contents

THE MODERN PERIOD (1900 to the Present)   83

                                                CD Tracks

DEBUSSY, Claude   84
    Reverie   [65] & [66]   85

SATIE, Erik   86
    Gymnopédie   [67] & [68]   87

JOPLIN, Scott   88
    The Entertainer   [69] & [70]   89

STRAVINSKY, Igor   90
    Petrouchka - Story of the Ballet   91
    Petrouchka   [71] & [72]   93

PROKOFIEV   94
    The Love for Three Oranges - Story of the Opera   95
    The Love for Three Oranges - March   [73] & [74]   97

Questions for Musical Prodigies - Modern Period   98

Good Listening from the Modern Period   99

APPENDICES

    [1] MUSICAL NOTATION OF THEMES   101

    [2] GLOSSARY   107

    [3] BIBLIOGRAPHY   111

INDEX OF CD TRACKS   112

INDEX OF COMPOSERS   113

INDEX OF COMPOSITIONS   114

CLASSICAL MAGIC'S®

CLASSICAL KARAOKE

for

KIDS

TIMELINE OF COMPOSERS

Giving a date to a period of history is always approximate. Some periods of music arrived earlier in one part of Europe than in another, and some composers spanned more than one period. The following is by no means a complete list of classical music composers. However, the most familiar names are included. The composers included in **CLASSICAL MAGIC's** *Classical Karaoke for Kids* appear in bold type.

BAROQUE PERIOD (c.1600 – 1750)
PACHELBEL, Johann	(1653 - 1706)
ALBINONI, Tomaso	(1671 - 1751)
VIVALDI, Antonio	(1678 - 1741)
MOURET, Jean-Joseph	(1682 - 1738)
BACH, Johann Sebastian	(1685 - 1750)
SCARLATTI, Domenico	(1685 - 1757)
HANDEL, George Frideric	(1685 - 1759)

CLASSICAL PERIOD (1750 - 1820)
GLUCK, Christoph	(1714 - 1787)
HAYDN, Franz Joseph	(1732 - 1809)
BOCCHERINI, Luigi	(1743 - 1805)
MOZART, Wolfgang	(1756 - 1791)
BEETHOVEN, Ludwig van	(1770 - 1827)
SCHUBERT, Franz	(1797 - 1828)

ROMANTIC PERIOD (1820 - 1900)
PAGANINI, Niccolò	(1782 - 1840)
WEBER, Carl Maria von	(1786 - 1826)
ROSSINI, Gioachino	(1792 - 1868)
BERLIOZ, Hector	(1803 - 1869)
MENDELSSOHN, Felix	(1809 - 1847)
CHOPIN, Frédéric	(1810 - 1849)
SCHUMANN, Robert	(1810 - 1856)
LISZT, Franz	(1811 - 1886)
WAGNER, Richard	(1813 - 1883)
VERDI, Giuseppe	(1813 - 1901)
GOUNOD, Charles	(1818 - 1893)
OFFENBACH, Jacques	(1819 - 1880)
SMETANA, Bedřich	(1824 - 1884)
STRAUSS, Johann Jr.	(1825 - 1899)
BRAHMS, Johannes	(1833 - 1897)
BORODIN, Alexander	(1833 - 1887)
PONCHIELLI, Amilcare	(1834 - 1886)
SAINT-SAËNS, Camille	(1835 - 1921)
DELIBES, Clement Léo	(1836 - 1891)
BIZET, Georges	(1838 - 1875)
MUSSORGSKY, Modest	(1839 - 1881)
TCHAIKOVSKY, Peter	(1840 - 1893)
DVOŘÁK, Antonin	(1841 - 1904)
SULLIVAN, Sir Arthur	(1842 - 1900)
MASSENET, Jules	(1842 - 1912)
GRIEG, Edvard	(1843 - 1907)
RIMSKY - KORSAKOV, Nicholas	(1844 - 1908)
FAURÉ, Gabriel	(1845 - 1924)
PUCCINI, Giacomo	(1858 - 1924)

MODERN PERIOD   (1900 to Present)

DEBUSSY, Claude   (1862 - 1918)
SOUSA, John Philip   (1854 - 1932)
ELGAR, Sir Edward   (1857 - 1934)
MAHLER, Gustav   (1860 - 1911)
STRAUSS, Richard   (1864 - 1949)
DUKAS, Paul   (1865 - 1935)
SIBELIUS, Jean   (1865 - 1957)
SATIE, Eric   (1866 - 1925)
JOPLIN, Scott   (1868 - 1917)
WILLIAMS, Ralph Vaughan   (1872 - 1958)
RACHMANINOFF, Sergei   (1873 - 1943)
HOLST, Gustav   (1874 - 1934)
SCHOENBERG, Arnold   (1874 - 1951)
IVES, Charles   (1874 - 1954)
RAVEL, Maurice   (1875 - 1937)
FALLA, Manuel de   (1876 - 1924)
BARTOK, Béla   (1881 - 1945)
ENESCO, Georges   (1881 - 1955)
STRAVINSKY, Igor   (1882 - 1971)
WEBERN, Anton   (1883 - 1945)
BERG, Alban   (1885 - 1935)
PROKOFIEV, Sergei   (1891 - 1953)
HINDEMITH, Paul   (1895 - 1963)
ORFF, Carl   (1895 - 1982)
GERSHWIN, George   (1898 - 1937)
COPLAND, Aaron   (1900 - 1990)
KHACHATURIAN, Aram   (1903 - 1978)
SHOSTAKOVICH, Dmitri   (1906 - 1975)
BARBER, Samuel   (1910 - 1981)
CAGE, John   (1912 - 1992)
BERNSTEIN, Leonard   (1918 - 1990)

BAROQUE

Forte and Piano Go Baroque

(c. 1600-1750)

Performing for Royalty

THE BAROQUE PERIOD (c.1600 – 1750)

PACHELBEL, Johann   (1653 - 1706)
BACH, Johann Sebastian   (1685 - 1750)
SCARLATTI, Domenico   (1685 - 1757)
HANDEL, George Frideric   (1685 - 1759)

In the **Baroque** (buh-ROKE) **Period** music was written mainly for the church or for royalty. The Baroque era was the beginning of almost all of the musical styles up to the present. Many forms of instrumental music were developed during this time. The **sonata, concerto, dance suite, theme and variation**, and early **symphony** all began during the Baroque Period. This period also saw the beginning of **ballet** as well as **opera** and **oratorio**.

Baroque period music and art had many frills and fancy ornaments. In music that means things like **trills** and **grace notes**. Baroque composers wanted their music to be very expressive, to show passionate emotions. Much Baroque music is **polyphonic** with two or more melodies or variations of melodies interwoven in repeated layers.

During the Baroque Period the violin family reached its highest development, and the violin became the queen of instruments. The organ and the harpsichord were the principal keyboard instruments. In about 1709 an Italian man named Bartolomeo Cristofori made a **pianoforte**. Like the harpsichord, it is played by pressing keys; unlike the harpsichord, the sound is produced by vibrating strings which have been struck by felt hammers. It can be played both softly (*piano*) and loudly (*forte*), and the tones can be sustained. Today we usually just call it a **piano**. In the Classical Period the piano became the principal keyboard instrument, and it has remained so until the present.

---

sonata - a composition for one or two solo performers in three or four movements
concerto - a composition for a full orchestra featuring a solo instrument
symphony - a composition for a full orchestra, usually in four movements
dance suite - a group of dances belonging to a set
theme and variation - a musical idea that is presented, then restated in various forms
ballet - a theatrical performance using ballet dancing to convey a story, theme, or atmosphere
opera - a musical **play** with orchestra in which most words are sung rather than spoken
oratorio - a musical **story** in which words are sung rather than spoken
trill - the quick repeating of two adjacent notes
grace note - an extra note played very quickly before the main note

JOHANN PACHELBEL
(1653 - 1706)

Johann Pachelbel (PAHKL-bell) was born in Nuremberg, Germany. He was a great organist and teacher. He was a friend of the Bach family and taught music to Johann Christoph Bach, the older brother of Johann Sebastian Bach. Johann Christoph later taught Johann Sebastian.

Pachelbel was a prolific composer for the organ, the harpsichord, and small instrumental groups. He was one of the greatest composers of organ **chorales** (kuh-RALS), which are hymn tunes or sacred melodies. Like Johann Sebastian Bach, he loved to experiment with elaborate variations on the chorale **fugue**. He composed more than seventy chorales and ninety fugues during his lifetime.

Pachelbel is best known for his **Canon in D**. It was originally written for three violins with bass. It has become very popular in many arrangements for different groups of instruments and keyboard.

A **canon** is similar to a round where two or more voices begin a melody at different times. You have probably sung *Brother John* (*Frére Jacques*) as a round.

---

chorale - a hymn tune, sacred melody
canon - a musical composition in two or more voice parts in which the melody is imitated exactly and completely by the successive voices
fugue - a fugue has one or two themes which are imitated by successively entering voices

Canon in D

Pachelbel
[1] & [2]

Pachelbel sing out your canon,
Pachelbel sing out your canon,
Pachelbel ring out your canon.

Pachelbel is ringing, singing.
Pachelbel is ringing, singing,
Bringing joy to all who listen
To his canon ringing, singing.

Pachelbel is ringing, singing.
Pachelbel is ringing, singing,
Ah…………

7

JOHANN SEBASTIAN BACH
(1685 - 1750)

Bach's father was a highly respected musician who played violin and viola. But Johann's father and mother both died before he was ten, so young Johann received very little systematic music training. However, he had such an interest in music and such hunger for learning that he copied, imitated, practiced, listened to, and experimented with any music he could find. He learned to play the organ, harpsichord, and violin. He once walked thirty miles from his town to Hamburg to hear a great organist play.

Johann worked very hard his entire life. It is said that a person copying his work by hand today, writing out all the parts as Bach did, would need seventy years to complete the task. Yet Bach wrote all his music while also serving as organist, conductor, and musical director of a church. (How many years did Johann Bach live?)

Bach never thought of himself as a genius, just a servant of the church composing his music for the glory of God. Many of his sons also became accomplished musicians. They, too, did not appreciate their father's genius. One of Bach's sons thought so little of his father's music that he sold some of his works for as little as ten cents apiece and negligently lost others.

Many organ works that Bach composed are still played today. We are very thankful that these compositions survived, as early manuscripts were often destroyed. They were sometimes even used to wrap the meat or butter from the market!

During his lifetime, Bach was better known as an organist than as a composer. He was one of the most skilled organists who ever lived. People would come from many miles to hear him play. Bach also improvised a lot of music that was never written down, much as jazz musicians do today. Unfortunately, we'll never be able to hear this music. Bach became ill in 1749 and became nearly blind. He died in 1750 after two unsuccessful operations on his eyes for cataracts.

The public forgot Bach's music for about 75 years. His music came at the end of the Baroque Period, and many people thought he was old-fashioned and stuffy. Felix Mendelssohn (Romantic Period) found Bach's great music almost a century after his death and brought it to the attention of the world. It has been loved ever since.

Bourrée II - Orchestral Suite No. 1

Bach
[3] & [4]

[: Peasants dancing, peasants laughing,
Peasants singing songs, peasants stomping grapes
To make some wine for Johann,
Johann Bach, Bach,
Playing his Bourrée while they work! :]

bourrée - one of the liveliest of the French court dances. The bourrée was a strong, vigorous dance, more suited to, and more popular with, the peasants than the nobility. Since the peasants danced in their wooden shoes, the music had to be strong and rhythmic in order to be heard above the clatter. In the wine-making regions of France the bourrée was a kind of work dance, the men singing and dancing as they crushed grapes with their bare feet.

Minuet in G

Bach
[5] & [6]

Bach wrote this little minuet.
I bet I never will forget!
I'll play my fiddle,
Play diddle, diddle,
You play the middle measure.

Bach wrote this little minuet.
I bet I never will forget!
I'll play my fiddle,
Play diddle, diddle,
Tell Bach I play by ear.

Bach, what a treasure!
Bach, play each measure.
Bach, what a pleasure
Waiting for me.
A B C D E F G
Play with me, I'm the best!

Play diddle dee, play diddle dum,
I'm having fun with Johann Bach.
D E F G A B C
Play with Johann Bach and me!

---

minuet - a slow, stately dance in triple meter (3 beats). It was introduced to the court during the Baroque Period and remained popular during the Classical Period. It evolved into the waltz of the Romantic Period.

Bach
[5] & [6]

Robin and Seth Parker playing with Johann Sebastian Bach.

Courante - Orchestral Suite No. 1   Bach
[7] & [8]

      I think that Johann Bach had many ears,
      Four to hear the oboes play,
      Four to hear the violins,
      And two to keep his wig in place
      And decorate his face!
      I have just two and
      Can't begin to hear it all,
          Can you?

I think that this courante is running wild!
Takes my breath away, I say,
Won't you come and dance
This running dance with me?
We'll count to three
And try to keep the beat.
This dancing hurts my feet!
I'd like to find a nice soft seat.

courante - a favorite dance at the French court from 1550 to 1750. Its name is the French word for "running." The courante was originally a dance in which the dancers leaped and ran. It started in Italy (as the *corrente*) and did not appear in France until the time of Catherine de' Medici's arrival there in 1530. From France it spread to England and Germany.

Harpsichord

The harpsichord is a plucked-string instrument played by pressing keys as in playing a piano. When the keys are pressed, small picks made of birds' quills or of hard leather pluck the strings. Harpsichord music has a twanging quality, and there is no way to play it louder or softer. The tones cannot be sustained. They die out almost immediately after being sounded.

Since the tones faded so quickly, Baroque performers would add musical **embellishments** called **ornaments** to fill the spaces. Ornaments are musical frills such as **grace notes**, **mordents**, **arpeggios** and **trills**.

> **embellishment** - a decoration
> **grace note** - an extra note played very quickly before the main note
> **mordent** - the written note quickly alternated with the note below it
> **arpeggio** - the notes of a chord played in order one at a time instead of together
> **trill** - the quick repeating of two adjacent notes

DOMENICO SCARLATTI
(1685 - 1757)

Three great musicians, Scarlatti, Bach and Handel were born in the same year. Bach and Handel were both born in Germany but Scarlatti was born in Italy. He was the sixth of ten children. Scarlatti's father, Alessandro, was the most important opera composer of his day. He trained Domenico, and by the age of sixteen Domenico was performing as organist in the royal chapel of Naples.

While Domenico Scarlatti was a professional organist, he played the harpsichord even better. Scarlatti and Handel admired each other greatly. Once they had a friendly contest on the organ and harpsichord. Handel was acknowledged as the master of the organ and Scarlatti of the harpsichord.

Scarlatti was born in Italy, but he spent many years in Portugal and Spain. He had accepted the post of music director at the Portuguese court in Lisbon. He taught the musically gifted Princess Maria Barbara to play the harpsichord. When Princess Maria married the heir to the throne of Spain, Scarlatti moved to Madrid with her. He spent the rest of his life at the court composing, teaching, and performing for this princess who became queen of Spain.

Scarlatti's amazing harpsichord playing dazzled his audiences much as Liszt's piano playing did a hundred years later. He was not well known in the rest of Europe until his works were discovered in the 1800's by virtuoso pianists who arranged them for the piano. His works are still very popular with pianists and audiences today.

Sonata in E, K. 380

Scarlatti
[9] & [10]

[: Harpsichord master, Scarlatti,
 Play a bit faster, Scarlatti. :]

Tra la la la la,
Hear the melody.
Hear the harmony,
This is Scarlatti.
Came from Italy,
Playing merrily
Sonata in E.

[: Handel and Bach and Scarlatti
 Handel and Bach and Scarlatti.
 Born in the same year were all three. :]

We'll be your friends forever,
We'll leave you not, no never.
Tra la la la la,
   la la la la ………

GEORGE FRIDERIC HANDEL
(1685 - 1759)

Handel was born in Germany the same year as Bach and Scarlatti. Bach spent most of his life close to his birthplace in Germany, but Handel had a great interest in the world. He spent time in Italy learning about Italian opera, and he lived most of his life in England.

Handel's father was a barber-surgeon. In his day the one with the cutting tools did double duty. He cut hair and whiskers or, if needed, he would perform surgery. A common practice in Handel's day was to cut a vein and "let" blood out. They thought they were letting the sickness drain out of the body!

Handel's father was sixty-three years old when Handel was born. The father had hoped that little George would become a lawyer, but George had other ideas. He loved music so much, and at seven played so well on the court chapel organ, that the duke convinced his father to let George study music. For three years he studied organ, harpsichord, oboe, violin, and composition. By the time he was eleven he was composing his own sonatas and church music.

The Italian style opera was very popular in Europe. Handel's friend, Johann Mattheson, composed operas. It is said that their friendship was firm but stormy. They once fought a duel over who was to play the harpsichord in certain parts of one of Mattheson's operas! Fortunately, neither man was hurt.

As you know from our studies of Handel, he wrote some of his most beautiful music, the *Water Music* and *Music for the Royal Fireworks,* for King George I and King George II of England. *The Messiah* was also written during his time in England. Handel liked England so much that he became a British citizen. He went blind six years before he died. He composed very little in those last six years. Although he asked for burial in Westminster Abbey "in a private manner," over 3,000 people attended his funeral. If you visit Westminster Abbey in London, England, be sure to look for his tomb.

The Harmonious Blacksmith was written for the harpsichord. It was composed for Anne and Caroline, the granddaughters of King George II. Anne and Caroline were Handel's pupils.

The Harmonious Blacksmith

Handel
[11] & [12]

Hear the blacksmith hammer his anvil,
Ringing like bells, Handel's harmony.
See the blacksmith hammer his anvil,
Muscles like iron, he's a sight to see.

    Sometimes it's forte,
    Now he plays it piano,
    Always singing as he's working,
    Hear the anvil ring.

"Come, good fellow,
I will fix your horse's shoe,
And if you wish,
I'll paint his toenails
   bright blue!"

17

QUESTIONS FOR THE MUSICAL PRODIGY - BAROQUE PERIOD

                                                                                                 Page

1. What is a prodigy?   (Look in the Glossary)   109
2. Which composer had many sons who were also accomplished musicians?   8
3. Who was known as the master of the harpsichord?   14
4. Which three Baroque composers were born in the same year?   2, 5, or 15
5. Who invented the piano? What nationality was he?   5
6. How did the pianoforte get its name?   5
7. How does a harpsichord differ from a piano?   13
8. What is an oratorio?   5
9. What famous composer had a duel over playing the harpsichord?   16
10. Whose music did Mendelssohn bring to the attention of the world?   8
11. What is an opera?   5
12. How many ears did Johann Bach have?   12
13. Which composer's father was a barber-surgeon?   16
14. What is a symphony?   5
15. Which composer was born in Italy but lived in Portugal and Spain?   14
16. In what country was Handel born?   16
17. The quick repeating of two adjacent notes is called a _____.   5
18. In which country did Handel spend most of his life?   16
19. Music with two or more interwoven melodies is called _____.   5
20. What is an arpeggio?   13
21. A symphony usually has how many movements?   5
22. Who once walked thirty miles to hear a great organist play?   8
23. Which composer was buried in Westminster Abbey in London?   16
24. Which composer's father was a barber-surgeon?   16
25. Who composed the Canon in D? (What is a musical canon?)   6
26. Which composer spent most of his life as a court musician in Spain?   14
27. How many instruments usually play a sonata?   5
28. Whose harpsichord compositions were later arranged for piano?   14
29. Which composer became blind six years before he died?   16
30. Whose music manuscripts were sometimes used to wrap meat and butter?   8
31. Which composer was better known as an organist than as a composer?   8
32. How can you tell a concerto from a symphony?   5
33. Who said he wrote only for the Glory of God?   8
34. Explain theme and variation.   5
35. The Baroque minuet evolved into what popular Romantic Period dance?   10
36. What is ballet?   5

To think about: Bach's sons did not appreciate their father's greatness. Others thought he was old-fashioned and stuffy! Is this an unusual problem? (p.8)

Good Listening from the Baroque Period

Vivaldi
- *The Four Seasons*
- Concerto for Two Trumpets in C Major
- Cello Concertos
- Flute Concertos
- Guitar and Mandolin Concertos

Bach

BWV numbers refer to the (thematic) catalog numbers of Bach's works.
- Violin Concertos, BWV 1041, 1042, 1043
- *English* Suites 1 - 6, (Piano) BWV 806-811
- *French* Suites 1 - 6, (Piano) BWV 812-817
- Oboe Concerto in D minor
- *Italian* Concerto in F, (Piano) BWV 971
- Sonatas and Partitas, Itzhak Perlman - violin, BWV 1001-1006
- *Goldberg Variations*

Bach's keyboard works can be played on either piano or harpsichord. Be sure to check which recording you are buying. Listen to some harpsichord music before you make your decision.

Handel
- Concerto Grosso, Opus 3, No. 1 - 6
- Concerto Grosso, Opus 6, No. 1 - 12
- Flute Sonatas, Opus 1, No. 7, 9, 11
- Harp Concerto in B Flat
- Violin Sonatas, Opus 1, No. 12, 13, 14
- Organ Concertos

Scarlatti
- Sonatas

Others
- Baroque Trumpet Music
- Pachelbel's Canon with Baroque Favorites

CLASSICAL

Piano and Forte Go Classical

(1750 - 1820)

Forte Posing as George Washington

THE CLASSICAL PERIOD (1750 -1820)

HAYDN, Franz Joseph   (1732 - 1809)
MOZART, Wolfgang Amadeus   (1756 - 1791)
BEETHOVEN, Ludwig van   (1770 - 1827)
SCHUBERT, Franz   (1797 - 1828)

Classical can be a confusing word. It refers both to a period of time and to a style of composition. In addition, all serious music by great composers is called classical music.

Classical Period - the musical period from 1750 to 1820.

Classical style - the style of music in the **Classical Period**.

Classical music refers to music that is more complex and lasts longer than popular music. It is not just music from the **Classical Period**. It includes music from four different periods: the Baroque, Classical, Romantic, and Modern. Each period has its own musical style. Music, art, and literature reflect the period in which they are produced.

The **Classical Period** was a time of change in ideas and feelings. Americans won their independence from England, and the social order in France was overthrown. In art, music, and literature, the people wanted a return to the simple beauties of nature and to clear thinking instead of fantasy. They were tired of the ornate Baroque style.

Music in the **Classical Period** was written for the rich upper classes, the aristocracy, rather than for the church. The nobleman wanted to hear music that was more reserved, controlled, elegant, and tuneful than the Baroque style. There were rules about the form of the music and how the themes were to be developed. Rather than having themes interwoven, the soprano line (the highest-pitched melody) dominated the composition.

Classical Period music featured contrast. The dynamics shifted frequently between piano and forte. One finds wide-ranging melodies with wide spaces between the bass and soprano. There is contrast in mood even within a movement. This is very different from the **Baroque Period** music, which was based on the idea of unity by repeating a motive or a fugue subject over a long harmonic plan with fewer dynamic contrasts or wide register spaces.

The Classical sonata form was the mold for the Classical music. Written in two, three or four movements, it was a perfect vehicle for contrasts and surprises.

Musical Forms of the Classical Period

form - Form in music means a musical plan similar to an outline for a book. Forms were well defined in the **Classical Period**. Form may refer to the <u>external form</u> of the music or <u>the form within the movements</u> of the music.

The **symphony, concerto, sonata** and **string quartet** were the prominent external forms in the **Classical Period**. To be a child prodigy (or an informed adult), you'll want to know how to tell them apart. Most, but not all, classical music compositions use the following form structure:

string quartet - composition for two violins, viola, and cello
      four movements   Fast Slow Minuet Fast

symphony - composition for a full orchestra
      four movements   Fast Slow Minuet Fast

    (**symphony** can also refer to the type of orchestra,
        i.e. a symphony orchestra)

concerto - composition for a full orchestra featuring a solo instrument
      three movements   Fast Slow Fast

sonata - composition for only one or two instruments
      usually three movements   Fast Slow Fast

sonata form - This designates the form <u>within</u> a movement rather than a total work. It is frequently used for single movements of sonatas, symphonies, quartets, and overtures. Since the sonata form is used most often in first movements, it is often known as *first-movement form* or *sonata allegro form.* A movement written in sonata form consists of three sections - exposition, development, and recapitulation, sometimes called statement, fantasia section, and restatement.

A **movement** is a distinct part of a musical composition, like a chapter in a book. The musicians will usually stop completely between movements. Don't clap until the end of the last movement, or you may find yourself clapping alone.

Did you notice that there are more Fast than Slow movements? We usually get bored sooner with slow things, but we still want contrast or change because we also get bored if everything is fast. The classical composers worked out a balance. About the time we get tired of the Fast movement they change to the Slow movement and give our minds a rest. Then, before we go to sleep, they wake us up again with a Fast movement.

SYMPHONY ORCHESTRA SEATING PLAN

FRANZ JOSEPH HAYDN
(1732 - 1809)

Joseph Haydn (HIGH-din), or "Papa Haydn," as Mozart called him, is also called the "Father of the Symphony." He composed 104 symphonies. His parents were amateur musicians who played several instruments and loved to sing. Little Haydn was very talented.

When Haydn was only six years old his parents sent him away to a church school, hoping to prepare him for the priesthood. He sang in the boys' choir there, and when he reached eight he was invited to sing in the boys' choir at St. Stephen's cathedral in Vienna. He also received instruction in voice, violin, and keyboard but little in general education other than a bit of Latin. Young Haydn wanted most of all to compose, but he received very little instruction. He was dismissed from the choir when he cut off the pigtail of the boy in front of him. Then almost seventeen, he earned a living by giving lessons and occasionally performing. He also studied composition and began composing. His music soon caught the attention of the royal family.

Haydn worked twenty-eight years as court musician for the Esterházy family of Austria. Although he was considered a "servant," he was treated well and was happy that he could devote himself entirely to music. Prince Esterházy was a music lover who appreciated Haydn's great talent. Since the Prince was his employer, Haydn wrote most of his music for the court. This included music for worship.

Prince Esterházy entertained lavishly, and Haydn wrote delightful music for the palace parties. With everyone dressed in finest apparel, parties were truly palace style shows. The food and entertainment were the best. Haydn and his orchestra played beautiful music for all to enjoy.

Haydn's marriage was not a happy one. His wife had little appreciation for his music. It is reported that she sometimes used strips of his manuscripts for curling her hair or lined her cake tins with his music sheets.

Haydn was famous and beloved all over Europe. He spent three years in London where he wrote his twelve *London* symphonies. These include: **No. 94,** the *Surprise;* **No. 101,** the *Clock;* **No. 103,** *Drum Roll;* and **No 104,** the *London,* his last symphony. You will find the *Surprise* and *London* in **Volumes 1** and **2** of *Themes to Remember.* In this volume you will learn all four movements of the *Clock* and the fourth movement of the *Drum Roll.*

The *Clock* Symphony No. 101
Movement 1 - *Adagio the Cat*

Haydn
[13] & [14]

Adagio the Cat loves mousey pie!
While he is sleeping
Little mousey is creeping
'Round his tail and toes.
Please don't touch his nose!

        Be careful, little mouse.
        Go, hide in Haydn's house.
            Adagio is mean!
            He's so mean
            He'll devour you!

        Go, hide in Haydn's house
            In the clock.

The *Clock* Symphony No. 101
Movement 1 - *Tickety Tock*

Haydn

[13] & [14]

Ta tickety, tickety, tock the clock,
Tock the clock,
Tickety tickety tock, tock.

Ta tickety, tickety, tock the clock,
Tock the clock,
Tickety, tickety, tickety tock.

Ta tickety, tickety, tock the clock,
Ta tickety, tickety tock.
Tick tock, tick tock.

The mouse is looking for the clock
In Haydn's house!
Mouse house, house mouse!

Movement 2 - *Hear the Clock Tick*

**Haydn
[15] & [16]**

Hear the clock tick,
There running goes the mouse.
He'll surely hide in Haydn's house,
For now the cat is coming.

The *Clock* Symphony No. 101
Movement 2 - *Mean Old Cat*

Haydn
[15] & [16]

Hear the clock tick,
There running goes the cat,
He'll surely find little mouse and
Eat him for his dinner,
Think of that,
That mean old cat!

Movement 2 - *Cat is Waiting*

Haydn
[15] & [16]

Cat is waiting, contemplating
Cogitating, calculating,
How he'll catch that yummy little mouse,
Yummy, yummy little mouse,
Yummy, yummy little mouse.

The *Clock* Symphony No. 101
Movement 2 - *Ears for Breakfast*

Haydn
[15] & [16]

He'll have ears for breakfast,
Feet for lunch and tail for brunch,
Oh yummy munch munch!

Movement 2 - *Watch Out*

Haydn
[15] & [16]

Watch out, little mousey!
Hide your whiskers
In your housey,
Tick tock housey,

Haydn's house
Will keep you safe
From hungry cats
And owls and bats, oh,

Hear the ticking, tocking, tocking.
Hear the clock tick,
There hiding is the mouse.
He'll surely stay in Haydn's house
Until the cat has gone,
But how his heart beats,
Shaking so and trembling with fear.

Still the cat is waiting,
Still he's calculating,
How he'll catch that little mousey
For his supper snack!

The *Clock* Symphony No. 101
Movement 3 - *Be Still Little Mouse*

Haydn
[17] & [18]

Be still little mouse,
Hiding in Haydn's house.
No peeking, no squeaking,
Cats think mice are nice!

    Be still little mouse,
    Hiding in Haydn's house
    In the clock, tick, tock,
    Ticking, ticking, ticking,
    Tocking, tocking, tocking,
    Hoping for the cat
    To weary of his waiting.

Go away, cat!
Your mother's calling you to come!
Come, come, come and eat your fish!

    Come, come,
    Eat your fish!

Forget the mouse!
Forget the mouse!

Movement 4 - *Cat's Going Home*

Haydn
[19] & [20]

Cat's going home,
So mousey's celebrating.
Cat's going home,
To eat his mother's fish!

    There he goes!
    There he goes!
    He's not happy!
       Go! Go!
    Eat your fishkin
    From your dishkin.

        Mousey's safe now!
        Thank you, Haydn,
        Thank you, Joe!

            Cat's going home,
            So mousey's celebrating.
              Cat's going home,
              To eat his mother's fish!

Adagio will never catch Allegro because Allegro is faster than Adagio.

The *Drum Roll* Symphony No. 103, Mvt. 4

Haydn
[21] & [22]

Haydn's Symphony.
Pa Pa Pa Haydn can roll his drum drum roll.
Pa Pa Pa Haydn can roll his drum drum roll.
Pa Pa Pa Haydn can rock,
Pa Pa Pa Haydn can roll his timpani……..

Pa Pa Pa Haydn,
Pa Pa Pa Haydn,
Pa Pa Pa Haydn,
Pa Pa Pa Pa,
His Symphony 103.

Pa Pa Pa Haydn can play his
Symphony 103 on timpani.
   Pa Pa Pa Haydn,
Yes Haydn, Pa Pa Haydn.

Pa Pa Pa Haydn can roll his drum drum roll,
Pa Pa Pa Haydn can roll his drum drum roll.
Pa Pa Pa Haydn can play his Symphony 103.
Pa Pa Pa Haydn, Pa Pa Pa Haydn,
Pa Pa Pa Haydn rocks and rolls his timpani.

Pa Pa Pa Haydn, Pa Pa Pa Haydn,
Pa Pa Pa **Pa,** Pa Pa Pa **Pa,**
Pa Pa Pa Haydn's 103.

Haydn
[21] & [22]

Papa Haydn's Drum Drum Roll

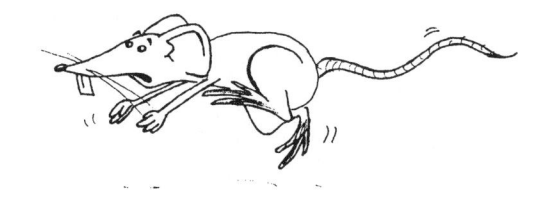

WOLFGANG AMADEUS MOZART
(1756 - 1791)

Wolfgang Amadeus Mozart (MOHT-sart): the most complete genius of all composers! He produced music more easily than most of us sing a song. He was a gifted pianist, violinist, and conductor. His "musical ear" was incredible. He could listen to complex music and later write it down totally from memory.

Mozart's father, also a musician, recognized his son's talent and provided him with early training. When he was eight he wrote his first symphony. His sister, Maria Anna (Nannerl), was also very talented. Papa Mozart took the children on tours to perform in Vienna, Paris, and London. They performed for the royalty of each country and were greeted as "wonder children." Wolfgang's ability to read any music at sight astounded everyone. He could also **improvise** brilliantly for hours.

Mozart was born in Salzburg, Austria. When he was a young man he moved to Vienna, the center of the classical music world. There he met "Papa Haydn." Haydn taught Mozart and they became very good friends. Although Haydn was much older, he learned from the brilliant Mozart. Haydn knew that a musical genius such as Mozart was truly rare.

In addition to instrumental music, Mozart wrote many operas. One of his most famous is ***Don Giovanni*** or ***Don Juan***. ***Don*** means "Mr." or "Sir." ***Juan*** is Spanish and ***Giovanni*** is Italian. Both mean ***John***.

Don Juan's goal in life was to love all the women in the world. However, this got him into BIG trouble! He killed the father of one woman. At the end of the opera, the ghost of the father, along with demons, came to claim ***Don Juan*** as their own and take him to his "home" in the underworld. (Wait until you grow up to watch this one!) But it won't hurt to sing Mozart's beautiful music.

Mozart died very young, at age thirty-five. However, during his short life he composed volumes of music. His music is the ultimate example of the classical style. It is gracious, elegant, and refined, yet it has a sense of divine inspiration. Mozart's middle name, *Amadeus,* means "beloved of God." When we listen to Mozart's music, we agree that he is "beloved of God."

> **improvise** - to make up new music on the spur of the moment

Minuet from *Don Juan*   **Mozart**
[23] & [24]

Don Juan loved all the pretty girls;
Mozart loved music
Better than the girls.
I like the girls and music, too,
But what is that to you?

Don Juan loved all the pretty girls;
Mozart loved music
Better than the girls.
I like the girls and music, too.
I'll bet that you do, too!

Piano Sonata in C, K. 545   [25] & [26]

Play, Mozart, play for me,
I really love Sonata in C.
Play, Wolfgang Mozart,
Wolfgang Mozart.

   Go, go Mozart,
   Go, go Mozart,
   Go, Wolfgang.

LUDWIG van BEETHOVEN
(1770 - 1827)

Beethoven (BAY-toe-ven) was born in Bonn, a little town on the banks of the Rhine River in Germany. His father was a poorly paid musician in the court orchestra. He could see that Ludwig had talent, and he gave the boy lessons on the piano and violin, hoping that Ludwig would be a child prodigy and make the family rich. Beethoven was a musical genius, but he never made a fortune for himself or his family. His father was an alcoholic who would stay up late drinking with his friends. It is said that he'd bring his friends home, wake up poor little Ludwig and make him play for them. If the young musician made a mistake, his father would box him on the ears. Perhaps this treatment contributed to Beethoven's deafness in later years.

Beethoven was the bridge between the Classical and the Romantic periods. His early music followed the classical rules of composition, but his later music was too dynamic to be restrained by rules. Emotions, from stormy passions to warm tenderness, began to take the place of elegant aristocratic rules in all the arts. The American and French revolutions were proclaiming the importance of every man, not just the nobility.

Für Elise is a favorite of piano students. Nobody knows for sure just who Elise was. One theory is that she was Therese Malfatti, the daughter of an Italian physician that Beethoven knew. Beethoven is said to have proposed to her but she married someone else. *Für Elise* was probably Therese, since the autographed score was at one time in her possession. I think that Elise was Beethoven's niece!

The **Turkish March** is from the incidental music for **The Ruins of Athens**, a play which was produced for the opening of a new theater in Budapest, Hungary in 1812. It begins softly and grows steadily louder as a procession nears, then grows steadily softer as it passes and disappears into the distance.

Beethoven's Fifth Symphony is perhaps the best known of the nine symphonies he wrote. You learned the theme of the first movement in **Volume 1** of *Themes To Remember* and themes for the second and third movements in **Volume 2** of *Themes To Remember.* In this volume you can learn the theme for the fourth movement. Now you can enjoy listening to the entire **Fifth Symphony**. You'll even know which movement you are hearing. Most adults can't do that!

Für Elise　　　　　　　　　　　　　　　　　　　　　　　**Beethoven**
　　　　　　　　　　　　　　　　　　　　　　　　　　　　[27] & [28]

　　　Lovely, lovely music for Elise,
　　　Beethoven's niece,
　　　She lived in Greece.
　　　Lovely, lovely music for Elise,
　　　Beethoven's niece,
　　　She loved this piece. (Fine)

　　　　　Oh she was kind,
　　　　　She was sweet.
　　　　　She wore mittens
　　　　　On her feet!
　　　　　　　(D.C. al Fine)

Turkish March from *The Ruins of Athens*   **Beethoven [29] & [30]**

Turks are marching,
Turks are marching,
Marching to the beat,
Beethoven's beat.
Turks are marching,
Turks are marching,
Marching to Beethoven's beat.
        Left foot forward,
        Left foot forward,
        Left foot, right foot,
        Left foot, right foot.
                Turks are marching,
                Turks are marching,
                Marching to the beat,
                Beethoven's beat.

Turks are marching,
Turks are marching,
Marching to Beethoven's beat.

Symphony No. 5, Movement 4

Beethoven
[31] & [32]

Beethoven, this is farewell, so long to the Fifth Symphony.
I like the first and second movements a whole bunch,
And Movement Three moves right along with lots of punch,
But Movement Four is best of all; I always sing it during lunch!

Tra la la la la, la la la la, la la la la.
Tra la la la la, la la la la, la la la la,

Symphony number five,
Makes my heart come alive,
Fills my soul with wonder and praise,
To God our voices we raise.
    We'll fly with the birds and
    Run with the wind,
    And shine like the sun….

La la la la, la la la la, la la la la
La la la la, la la la la,
   La la la la, la la la la…

FRANZ SCHUBERT
(1797 - 1828)

Franz Schubert (SHOE-bert) was another musical genius. He was born in Vienna, Austria, the center of the music world in the Classical Period. Like Mozart, he turned out volumes of beautiful melodies. His father was a school master who thought that Franz should follow in his footsteps. Papa Schubert was a practical man who probably believed that it was better to make a small salary as a teacher than to starve as a musician. Father Schubert played the cello and gave Franz lessons on the violin and piano, but he still thought that Franz should be a teacher! To please his father, Franz tried teaching for a while, but he was unable to keep discipline and he hated this career. His father finally agreed that Franz would be happier composing than teaching.

Schubert was so talented that one of his teachers said, "I can't teach him anything else. He's learned it all from God himself!" While he was not a **virtuoso** pianist like Mozart or Beethoven, he loved evenings of playing piano for his friends. These evenings became known as *Schubertiads.*

Schubert was born to create, to compose beautiful music, and that he did. He wrote nine symphonies, but he was best at writing small piano pieces called *impromptus*, *moments musicals,* or *serenades*. Schubert is especially known for his songs called *Lieder* (LEE-der) in German. He wrote very quickly, sometimes eight songs in a single day, and over 600 songs in the thirty-one years of his brief life. He also wrote many compositions for strings: **quartets, quintets** and **trios**.

> **virtuoso** - a performer who excels on his or her instrument
> **quartet** - a composition for four instruments or voices
> **quintet** - a composition for five instruments
> **piano quintet** - usually consists of a piano and a
>   **string quartet** (which has two violins, one viola, and one cello)
> **trio** - music written for three instruments or voices
> **impromptu** - a short musical composition which seems improvised
> **moment musical** - a musical moment, a Schubert idea
> **serenade** - evening music, vocal or instrumental

Serenade, Op. 90, No. 11   Schubert [33] & [34]

Sing Serenade
The one Schubert played,
The night he sang to the stars.
(Night he sang to the stars.)

Angels above
Still sing of God's love,
For all his children on earth.
(For all his children on earth.)

    [: Peace they bring,
        Come let us sing
        This serenade of love,
        Love that brings peace on earth. :]

QUESTIONS FOR THE MUSICAL PRODIGY - CLASSICAL PERIOD

	Page
1. Which composer played before royalty as a small child?	36
2. Which music period had many composition rules to follow?	21
3. Who was sent away to school when he was only six years old?	24
4. What does Amadeus mean?	36
5. What is a virtuoso?	42
6. In the Classical Period, for whom was most of the music written?	21
7. In the orchestra seating, which instruments are in the left front section?	23
8. Who was called the "Father of the Symphony"?	24
9. For the Classical Period, Forte wears a hat like which early American?	20
10. Who's father boxed him on the ears when he played wrong notes?	38
11. How many instruments play in a quartet? A quintet?	42
12. Which music is more complex and lasts longer---popular or classical?	21
13. What instrument is Haydn playing in the *Drum Roll* Symphony?	34
14. In the orchestra seating, who is seated in the right front section?	23
15. Who worked many years for Prince Esterházy?	24
16. Who liked to play for his friends in musical evenings?	42
17. How many movements does a symphony usually have?	22
18. Which movement is the slow movement in a Classical symphony?	22
19. In Haydn's *Clock* Symphony, what is the cat's name? The mouse?	25
20. What do Adagio and Allegro mean?	(Glossary)
21. In the symphony orchestra seating, where are percussion instruments?	23
22. Who lived in London for a time and wrote the "London" symphonies?	24
23. In which music is it easier to hear a melody---Classical or Baroque?	21
24. In Haydn's *Clock* Symphony, what did the cat's mother tell him to do?	32
25. What is a movement in a musical composition?	22
26. Where are the woodwinds seated in the symphony orchestra?	23
27. Who was dismissed from a choir for cutting off a boy's pigtail?	24
28. Which composer wrote beautiful music even after he was deaf?	38
29. Which composer is especially known for songs called *Lieder*?	42
30. What does it mean to improvise?	36
31. How many symphonies did Haydn compose?	24
32. How many symphonies did Beethoven compose?	38
33. How does a concerto differ from a symphony?	22
34. Who took lessons from Haydn and called him "Papa Haydn"?	36
35. What is a string quartet? Which instruments would usually play?	22
36. Rather than interwoven themes, what dominates Classical music?	21
37. In a symphony orchestra setting, where are the brass instruments?	23

To think about: Do you think children should be sent away to school when they are six years old?

Good Listening from the Classical Period

Haydn
    Symphony No. 104 in D (*London*)
    Symphony No. 94 in G (*Surprise*)
    Symphony No. 103 in E Flat (*Drum Roll*)
    String Quartets - Haydn wrote many--all good listening
        Quartet in B Flat, Op. l, No. 1 (*The Hunt*)
        Quartet in D, Op. 64, No. 5 (*Lark*)
        Quartet in C, Op. 76, No. 3 (*Emperor*)
    Piano Sonatas - (Lovely light listening)
    Piano Trios - (Piano, violin and cello)

Mozart
K stands for Köchel (KER-shell) who made a chronological list of more than 600 musical works by Mozart.
    Sonata in B Flat - Violin and Piano, K. 378
    The Magic Flute - Opera
    Violin Concerto in G, K. 216
    Piano Concerto No. 21 in C, K. 467
    Eine Kleine Nachtmusik - Serenade in G, String Orchestra, K. 525
    Quartets, Sonatas, Serenades, and Symphonies
        Mozart is the ultimate in good listening.

Beethoven
    Piano Concerto No. 1 in C
    Piano Concerto No. 2 in B Flat
    Piano Concerto No. 3 in C minor
    Piano Sonatas
      (*Pathetique, Moonlight, Waldstein, Appassionata, Hammerklavier*)
    Symphony No. 6 in F (*Pastoral*)
    Symphony No. 9 in D minor (*Choral*)
    Symphonies No. 5 & 7
    String Quartets
    Violin Romance No. 1 and No. 2

Schubert
    Impromptus, Op. 90, No. 1 - 4
        Op. 142, No. 1 - 4
    Moments Musicals, Op. 94, No. 1 - 6
    Military Marches (Four hands), Op. 51, No. 1 - 3
    String Quartet in D Minor (*Death and the Maiden*)

ROMANTIC

Piano and Forte Go Romantic

(1820 - 1900)

Forte Posing as Abraham Lincoln

THE ROMANTIC PERIOD (1820 - 1900)

MENDELSSOHN, Felix	(1809 - 1847)
CHOPIN, Frédéric	(1810 - 1849)
WAGNER, Richard	(1813 - 1883)
VERDI, Giuseppe	(1813 - 1901)
OFFENBACH, Jacques	(1819 - 1880)
SMETANA, Bedřich	(1824 - 1884)
STRAUSS, Johann Jr.	(1825 - 1899)
BRAHMS, Johannes	(1833 - 1897)
PONCHIELLI, Almilcare	(1834 - 1886)
TCHAIKOVSKY, Peter	(1840 - 1893)

The Romantic Period is very different from the Classical Period. The Romantic composer stressed the dignity and freedom of man, an idealized nature, the rustic village, the hero-warrior, warm lush sounds, and emotions. The Classical Period had stressed control of form and emotions.

Music, literature, and art reflect the periods in which they are produced. The music of the **Baroque** Period was written mainly for the church or the court. The **Classical** composer wrote principally for the rich upper classes, the aristocracy. The **Romantic** composer wrote for the rising middle class. His music was a passionate expression of personal feelings and thoughts, not just entertainment. He needed to make a living from his music by sales or by performance. Composers, such as Paganini on the violin and Liszt and Chopin on the piano, performed brilliantly for their audiences. New instruments and the improvement of existing instruments gave the orchestras a richer, warmer, more powerful sound.

During the Romantic Period, the forms of music were varied. Chopin wrote dazzling short works: waltzes, preludes, fantasies (*Fantasie-Impromptu*) and études (*Tristesse* **Étude**) for the piano. Liszt wrote emotional rhapsodies and concertos. Brahms wrote dark-hued symphonies. Tchaikovsky brought the ballet into prominence. Two themes from his ballets, ***Sleeping Beauty*** and ***Romeo and Juliet***, are included in this volume. The waltz replaced the minuet. Symphonic poems (or tone poems) were popular. With music they "painted" storms, sunrises, and life with idealized nature. Smetana's *Moldau* is a tone poem. Offenbach (***Orpheus and Eurydice***) and Sullivan wrote light-hearted operettas while Wagner (VOGG-ner) wrote a huge four-opera set, *Ring of the Nibelungs,* about Norse gods, giants, a dragon, and enchantment. The ***Ride of the Valkyries*** is from that opera.

During the Romantic Period, many composers were conscious of their national heritage. Chopin, Grieg, Dvořák, Smetana, Debussy, Mussorgsky, and Borodin used the folk melodies of their native lands in their music.

FELIX MENDELSSOHN
(1809 - 1847)

Felix Mendelssohn (MEN-dl-son) came from a wealthy family that nurtured his musical talent. He did not have to deal with the financial struggles that plagued many of the great masters. His father was a Jewish banker, grandson of the noted philosopher, Moses Mendelssohn. The family converted to Christianity, adding the gentile name, Bartholdy, to distinguish their family from the unconverted Mendelssohns.

Felix was given the best of educations including violin, piano, viola, and composition. He was almost as talented as Mozart. Like Mozart, he could compose music fully formed in his head and then write it down. He also had a wonderful musical memory.

Mendelssohn is responsible for bringing Bach's music to light. Bach had been a famous organist, but he was not widely known outside of Germany in his own lifetime. After his death in 1750, his music was almost forgotten until Felix found it a century later and brought it to the attention of the world. Bach's music has been loved and played around the world ever since.

Mendelssohn composed wonderful symphonies and concertos. He wrote just one concerto for the violin, as did Beethoven and Tchaikovsky. He also wrote an oratorio called *Elijah*. Remember that an oratorio is a musical story with chorus, soloists, and orchestra. It is usually based on the Bible.

The ***Spring Song*** is one of the most popular pieces that Mendelssohn ever wrote. It is included in a collection of forty-eight pieces called ***Songs Without Words.*** They are related to **tone poems** but shorter. They are described as "an instrumental piece that has the vocal and lyrical character of a song." They are impressions caught in music of great charm and originality.

Like Mozart, Mendelssohn died very young. He was only 38 years old. The death of his beloved sister, Fanny, a gifted composer and pianist, was a great blow to him. His health failed, and he began to have small strokes followed by a massive stroke. He died in 1847, the same year as Fanny. He was buried in Berlin.

Spring Song, Op. 62, No. 6   **Mendelssohn**
[35] & [36]

James and Sean Quick enjoying Mendelssohn's *Spring Song*

Don't you love to sing
This Spring Song, Mendelssohn?
The birds all sing a wing song,
Bees all buzz their honey sting song.
So when you smell a flower,
Better watch your nose!
For every bee just loves to zing
    His sting song!

FRÉDÉRIC CHOPIN
(1810 - 1849)

Frédéric Chopin (sho-PAN) was born in Poland. His mother was Polish and his father French. Frédéric left Poland when he was twenty and made his home in France for the rest of his life. However, he never forgot his Polish heritage. His music is full of the sounds of Polish national dances such as the mazurka and polonaise. Chopin's *Revolutionary* Étude and *Military Polonaise* reflect his nationalism and his distress with the Russian occupation of Poland.

Chopin never married, but he fell in love with a famous French novelist, George Sand. George was a woman, but she wore men's clothing and smoked cigars. She was the very opposite of Chopin, who was frail and wore elegant clothing! She probably chose a man's name to help sell her books. Her real name was Amandine Aurore Lucie Dupin! Perhaps that's why she changed her name to George!

Most of Chopin's compositions were short works for the piano. There are **preludes, études, nocturnes, waltzes, mazurkas, polonaises, impromptus,** and **sonatas**. (Terms are defined in the Glossary.) He composed in many moods: tragic, sweet, dreamy, brilliant, heroic, fantastic, and simple. He was the master of beautiful melody. Many of his melodies have been used in popular songs. The theme from the ***Cantabile*** of ***Fantasie-Impromptu*** was once a popular song called *I'm Always Chasing Rainbows*. The **Tristesse** **Etude** melody was popular as *No Other Love*.

Chopin was a brilliant pianist. He enthralled people with his wonderful music, and he was in great demand to perform. However, he was frail and sickly, so he limited his public appearances. He usually played for small groups in elegant French homes. During this time, Liszt was the only other composer who rivaled Chopin in his virtuosity. (A **virtuoso** is someone who can play amazingly well.)

The last concert Chopin performed was a benefit for Polish refugees. He was only thirty-nine when he died. Mozart's *Requiem* was played at his funeral as Chopin had requested. An urn of Polish soil, given to him by his music teacher when he left Poland, was buried with him.

> **impromptu** - a composition of the Romantic Period (the name implies a somewhat casual origin of the piece in the composer's mind)
> **étude** - a study, a piece aimed at teaching a musical skill

Cantabile from *Fantasie-Impromptu*, Op. 66

Chopin
[37] & [38]

Chopin is chasing rainbows,
Fantasie-Impromptu,
Come, chase the clouds and rainbows, too.
Come, fly among the stars.
Chopin is chasing rainbows,
Fantasie-Impromptu,
Come, sing **Cantabile** with me;
Great music sets us free!

cantabile - (cahn-TAH-bi-lay) Italian word - in a singing manner, singable

Tristesse Ètude in E, Op. 10, No. 3   **Chopin** [39] & [40]

No other love, Chopin, Chopin,
Can fill my heart, Chopin, Chopin.
No other love can take
This sadness from my life.
    Since you have gone,
        All my days are filled with sorrow,
        Life has ceased.
Tomorrow fears, tomorrow tears.
No other love, Chopin, Chopin,
Can fill my heart, Chopin, Chopin.
No other love……

tristesse - a French word that means sadness

Chopin performs for Piano and Forte

RICHARD WAGNER
(1813 - 1883)

Richard Wagner (REEKH-art VOGG-ner) is one of the biggest names in opera. He was born in Leipzig, Germany, but lived in many places in Europe. He married Liszt's daughter, Cosima. He believed that he was the greatest musician who had ever lived and one of the greatest poets, dramatists, and intellects of his generation. He was arrogant and had little consideration for anyone but himself. His personal life is not one to be imitated.

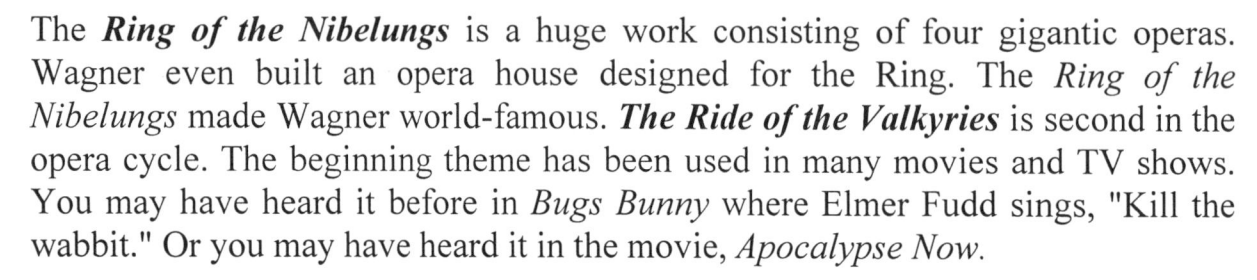

He had many failures in his early years, but his persistence and confidence in himself produced opera unlike any that had ever been produced before. It was huge in scope with music that is lush, powerful, imaginative, beautiful, and intense.

The **Ring of the Nibelungs** is a huge work consisting of four gigantic operas. Wagner even built an opera house designed for the Ring. The *Ring of the Nibelungs* made Wagner world-famous. **The Ride of the Valkyries** is second in the opera cycle. The beginning theme has been used in many movies and TV shows. You may have heard it before in *Bugs Bunny* where Elmer Fudd sings, "Kill the wabbit." Or you may have heard it in the movie, *Apocalypse Now*.

The operas are based on German and Norse mythology. They involve gods, giants, half-gods, earth-dwellers, and inhabitants of the underworld. Both **Wotan**. (VO-tahn), the King of the gods, and Alberich, ruler of the Nibelungs in the underworld, want complete power and wealth. The Ring is forged from gold stolen by Alberich from the Rhine maidens. It will make its owner all-powerful. Wotan steals the Ring from Alberich who places a curse on it. The rest of the opera deals with the conflict of good and evil and the struggle for possession of the Ring.

Valhalla (Vol-HALL-ah) is the home of **Wotan** and his twelve daughters who are called **Valkyries** (Val-KEER-ees). Brünnhilde is Wotan's favorite daughter and the most important of the Valkyries. The Valkyries carry the dead heroes to Valhalla. The heroes help them defend Valhalla in case of war with the Nibelungs. The Valkyries wear helmets and special armor and ride on flying horses.

Wagner is famous for his creation of the *Leitmotif* (LIGHT-mo-teef), which means "leading theme." He uses specific short themes to identify people, things, or moods. For instance, Wotan and Alberich each have a distinctive short theme of their own. Any time one of them appears, the orchestra plays his theme.

The Ride of the Valkyries

Wagner
[41] & [42]

Ride Valkyries, ride Valkyries,
Daughters of Wotan, with Wagner ride!
Ride to Valhalla, ride to Valhalla,
Daughters of Wotan, with Wagner ride!
With Wagner ride, with Wagner ride.
Go, choose the heroes, those who must die!
Take all the brave to meet the gods,
Take all the brave men,
Those who will love and defend Paradise.

GIUSEPPE VERDI
(1813 - 1901)

Giuseppe Verdi (VAIR-dee) is known as "Mr. Opera." He produced the most high quality operas of any composer. His melodies are beautiful and memorable. During his lifetime all Italy was singing Verdi melodies. He was born to a poor family in a tiny Italian village. A wealthy shopkeeper in a nearby town loved music and paid for Verdi's music education. Verdi later married the shopkeeper's daughter. His wife and two children all died within a short period. Verdi was devastated, but a good friend, from La Scala opera house in Milan, begged Verdi to overcome his grief and write an **opera**. That opera was *Nabucco,* a name for Nebuchadnezzar (NE-buh-kud-NEZ-er), the Babylonian king who conquered Jerusalem and exiled the Jews to Babylon in 586 B.C. Italy saw the Jews as a symbol of oppressed Italians. The **Chorus of Hebrew Slaves** from *Nabucco* became an Italian cry for independence and freedom. It made Verdi famous.

Aïda (ah-EE-duh) is Verdi's most popular opera. The ruler of Egypt asked Verdi to compose an opera for the opening of a new opera house in Cairo. It had been built to celebrate the opening of the Suez Canal in 1869. Aïda is one of the best loved operas ever written, but it is expensive to produce with spectacular processions and gigantic sets.

Verdi wrote many other operas which are still very popular with **operaphiles**. You may have learned the lyrics for *Rigoletto* in **Volume 2** of *Themes To Remember*. Verdi operas have beautiful **arias**. Operas also include **choral singing** and singing that is almost like talking which is called **recitative** (think of recite). The written words of an opera are called the **libretto**.

---

opera - a musical play with orchestra, chorus, solos, and people in costume who sing, rather than speak, their lines
operaphile - (a new word!) **phile** - means having a great liking for or attraction to something. An operaphile is one who has a strong attraction to opera.
aria - an elaborate melody sung by a single voice as in an opera or oratorio
libretto - the words of an opera or an oratorio
recitative - (res-uh-tuh-TEEV) music which sounds almost like speaking

Nabucco - Story of the Opera

Verdi
[43] & [44]

Nabucco (Nuh-BOO-koh) is based on the Old Testament story of Nebuchadnezzar (NEB-uh-kud-NEZ-er) who destroyed Jerusalem and took the Jews into exile to Babylon in 586 B.C.

Characters:
  Nabucco - the King of Babylon
  Fenena - a princess, the daughter of Nabucco
  Abigaille - a slave, believed to be a daughter of Nabucco
  Ismaele - the nephew of the King of Jersualem (the Jews or Hebrews)
  Zaccaria - High Priest of Jerusalem
  Jehovah - Another name for God

Act 1 - Ismaele has just brought the news that Nabucco, King of Babylon, is advancing toward Jerusalem. The Hebrews know that Nabucco plans to destroy their Holy Temple. Nabucco's daughter, Fenena, has been captured by the Hebrews, and Ismaele, son of the Hebrew king, has fallen in love with her.

Abigaille, a supposed sister of Fenena, has also come to Jerusalem. She is jealous of Fenena. She loves Ismaele and tells him that she has it in her power to seize the throne from Nabucco and to save Ishmael's life.

Zaccaria, the Hebrew High Priest, enters saying that Nabucco is at the city gates. Nabucco rides to the door of the Holy Temple. Zaccaria threatens to kill Nabucco's daughter, Fenena, if Nabucco sacks the Temple. Nabucco just laughs. Zaccaria attempts to kill Fenena but Ismaele stops him. Ismaele is considered a traitor for helping the enemy. Nabucco destroys the Temple.

Act 2 - The Hebrews (Jews) are taken captive to Babylon. Fenena is left in Jerusalem to reign in Nabucco's place. Abigaille discovers that she is a slave child rather than Nabucco's daughter, but she is determined to seize the throne and marry Ismaele. The Hebrews curse Ismaele as a traitor. However, Zaccaria reminds the Hebrews that Ismaele has converted Fenena to their faith and she is now their friend.

Nabucco - Story of the Opera

Verdi
[43] & [44]

The Babylonian priests spread the rumor that Nabucco has been killed in battle, but just as Abigaille is about to kill Fenena and take power, Nabucco walks in the door and seizes the crown, placing it on his own head. He proclaims that he is God! There is a clap of thunder, and the crown is torn from his head by a supernatural force. The King goes mad, and Abigaille seizes the crown!

Act 3 - Abigaille taunts Nabucco into signing a death sentence for the Jews. She puts both Nabucco and Fenena in prison. Meanwhile, we see the Jews as slaves in Babylon singing sadly about their homeland, their former glory, and their desire to go back home to Jerusalem. **(Chorus of Hebrew Slaves***)*

Act 4 - Nabucco hears the crowds shouting, "Death to Fenena." He sees her being led to execution. Nabucco prays to Jehovah to forgive his sin of pride and to spare Fenena's life. The prison guards free Nabucco. He reaches the place of execution just in time to save Fenena. The false idols tumble down. Nabucco and the Jews praise Jehovah. Abigaille has taken poison and she dies.

Nabucco - Overture

Verdi
[43] & [44]

Chorus of Hebrew Slaves

Thoughts of homeland, fly away.
Greet the banks of Jordan's lovely stream.
Thoughts so dear but so full of grief and sadness.
Toppled towers, **Zion** crushed.
Fatherland, so lovely and so lost.
Free us, Lord, from oppression
Or give us the strength for our sorrows to bear.

Golden harp, play your song,
Tell of good times,
Times long ago,
Times of home,
Times of peace,
Times of glory.
Memories give us hope,
Hope for new life
In our own land.
Praise our God, Jehovah,
Restore our home.

Toppled towers, Zion crushed,
Fatherland, so lovely and so lost!
Free us, Lord, from oppression
Or give us the strength for our sorrows to bear.

Save us, O Lord.
Lead us back to our home.
Save us, O Lord,
Lead us back to our home.

> **Zion** refers to Temple but also to Jerusalem and the Jewish people.
> (Lyrics are adapted from Verdi's libretto.)

Giuseppe VERDI   (1813 - 1901)

Aïda - Story of the Opera

The Ethiopian army is advancing toward the ancient capital of Egypt. Radames (RAH-duh-mees) is chosen to lead the Egyptian army against the Ethiopian invaders. He loves Aïda, the slave girl of the Egyptian princess, Amneris. The only problem is that both Aïda and Princess Amneris love Radames. Can you see trouble coming?

Radames leads the Egyptian army to victory against the Ethiopian invaders and returns to the capital in great procession with prisoners, soldiers, trumpets, and elephants to the strains of the ***Triumphal March***. Among the prisoners is the leader of the Ethiopians who just happens to be Aïda's father. He is dressed as a common soldier and warns Aïda to keep his identity secret.

As a reward for his victory against the Ethiopians, the Egyptian king promises Radames his daughter, Princess Amneris, in marriage. Radames, however, wants to marry Aïda, her slave, instead of the princess, but he doesn't dare to speak out.

Aïda and Radames plan a secret meeting by the moonlit Nile. While Aïda is waiting for Radames, her father appears. He tells Aïda that she must learn from Radames the secrets of his next battle plans against their people. Aïda is torn between loyalty to her father and her love for Radames. She knows that her father and her people may be killed by the army of Radames in the next battle.

The father hides and Radames appears. Aïda suggests that they run away together. Radames proposes that they leave by the unguarded pass his army plans to use the next day. Aïda's father hears the secret and comes out of hiding. Radames knows that he has been tricked, and he turns himself in for having aided the enemy.

Radames is sentenced to die in a tomb by himself. Princess Amneris wants to save him, but all the other Egyptians think he is a traitor. Aïda decides to hide in the tomb before they seal it. After Radames is sealed in the tomb, Aïda comes to his side, and they are united in death. Princess Amneris mourns for Radames above the tomb.

The *Triumphal March* from *Aïda*

Verdi
[45] & [46]

Verdi, Verdi the operaphile,
Told tales of tragic guile
Set on Egypt's Nile.
Aïda, Aïda, Aïda!
Verdi tells of brave Radames,
Sealed in the tomb alive.
Who is by his side? Aïda!
Radames sleeps by the Nile,

Sealed in the tomb alive,
Sealed in the tomb alive,
Sealed in the tomb to die,
Tomb to die, to die, to die, to die.
Verdi tells of brave Radames,
Sealed in his tomb alive.
Who is by his side?
Aïda, Aïda, sleeps by the Nile.

JACQUES OFFENBACH
(1819 - 1880)

Jacques Offenbach (zhak OFF-en-bahkh) was born in Cologne, Germany, to Jewish parents. His father, Isaac Judah Eberst, had come from the city of Offenbach. He was so often referred to as "Isaac der Offenbacher" that he decided to change his name to Offenbach. He taught singing and various instruments. When Jacques was six he started studying violin. He studied cello secretly because his parents thought he was too frail to play such a big instrument. One day the cello player in the family performance of a Haydn quartet failed to appear, and little Jacques startled his family by taking the seat and playing the cello part! They let him take cello lessons, and he became a part of the family trio which played in restaurants.

Jacques' father realized that his son was very talented and took him to Paris to study at the Conservatory. Jacques preferred playing light-hearted music in the Opéra-Comique orchestra. Then he decided that he'd like to compose his own operas. They were shorter and funnier than the serious operas that were in style. Unlike "grand opera," Offenbach's operas also include talking. More like Broadway musicals than traditional operas, they are called **operettas.**

Offenbach realized his dream of starting his own theater. He featured comic opera. He called it *Bouffes-Parisiens*. (*Bouffe* is French for buffoon, or clown.) He often made fun of the serious operas. His theater became immensely popular. His music was sung in the streets. He made people laugh and they loved him. ***Orpheus in the Underworld*** is one of his funniest operas. The famous ***Can Can*** dance came from this opera. Offenbach made fun of the "grand opera" versions of the Orpheus and Eurydice story from Greek mythology. His version is rather like a "Saturday Night Live" show.

Offenbach composed one serious opera, ***The Tales of Hoffmann,*** which remains a success even today. You will find the ***Barcarolle*** from that opera in ***Themes To Remember,*** **Volume 2.**

Can Can from *Orpheus in the Underworld*

Offenbach
[47] & [48]

Look! Offenbach can Can Can,
You can do the Can Can
Better than a man can.
You can kick much higher,
Kick higher than a rainbow,
Higher than a dodo.
They all kicked the bucket
Long ago-go!

The Greek myth of *Orpheus and Eurydice*

Offenbach [49] & [50]

Orpheus was the son of Apollo and Calliope. Apollo was the Greek god of sunlight, music and poetry, and Calliope was the Muse of poetry. When Orpheus was young his father gave him a lyre and taught him to play it. He became the most famous of musicians. Both humans and wild beasts were softened by his music. Even the trees and rocks were sensitive to the charm of his singing.

His music won the heart of Eurydice and they were married. At the wedding the torch smoked and brought tears to their eyes. This was a very bad omen.

Shortly after her marriage, Eurydice was seen by a shepherd who was struck by her beauty and tried to capture her. As she ran from him, she stepped on a poisonous snake. It bit her and she died. Orpheus was heart-broken. He sang of his sorrow to all who would listen. Finally, in his despair, he decided to descend into Hades, the underworld, to find Eurydice. He passed through crowds of ghosts and stood before the throne of Pluto. With his lyre he sang of his loneliness and begged for the return of Eurydice. His music was so sweet that everyone stopped to listen. Even the cheeks of the **Furies** were wet with tears.

Pluto was so moved that he called Eurydice. She came from among the newly arrived ghosts, limping with her wounded foot. Orpheus was permitted to take her away with him under one condition. He was not allowed to turn around and look at her until they reached the upper air. He led and Eurydice followed. They passed through the horrors of Hades, and Orpheus did not look back.

When they were past the dangers of the Underworld, Eurydice suddenly took hold of Orpheus. This startled him and he looked back at her. Eurydice was again lost to him, and this time there was no way to bring her back. At his death the nightingale sang sweetly over his grave. Jupiter placed his lyre among the stars. But the ghost of Orpheus passed again to the underworld to find his Eurydice.

Orpheus in the Underworld

Offenbach
[49] & [50]

Offenbach told me--
Orpheus made a trip to Hades,
Tried to get Eurydice,
He turned around and looked at her,
He should have known
The **Fates** would seize her!
What a stupid thing to do,
To lose his wife Eurydice.
All the music in the world
Won't bring her back - Eurydice.
[: Stupid Orpheus! Lost his wife Eurydice! :]

Furies - minor female gods who punished crimes on behalf of the victims of those crimes
Fates - three goddesses of destiny - they decided what happened to people

BEDŘICH SMETANA
(1824 - 1884)

Bedřich Smetana (BED-zhrikh SMEH-ta-nah) was from Bohemia, now the Czech Republic. He brought attention to the music of the young Dvořák, also from Bohemia and also interested in the folk songs of his people. (Remember Dvořák's *New World Symphony* in *Themes To Remember, Volume 1*.)

One of Smetana's most famous and appealing compositions is a set of six **tone poems** called *Má Vlast (My Fatherland)*. The **Moldau** (or *Vltava* in Czech) is the name of the mighty river that runs through much of the country.

The music begins with two solo flutes that represent the two mountain streams that form the source of the river. As the river grows, so does the sound of the orchestra. Instruments enter one after the other until one hears a mighty river of sound. The river flows through woods where hunting horns are heard. Onward it goes through fields, past a peasant wedding celebration and water nymphs at play. It passes over rapids and on through the great city of Prague. Smetana's music, like that of Dvořák's, catches the flavor of the Bohemian people. The melodies are so singable that they linger in our ears.

The Bartered Bride is the best known of the several operas Smetana wrote. It includes polkas, lush melodies and choruses. It won the heart of the Czech people and is still a favorite of opera audiences.

Smetana was very influential in the Czech movement for freedom from foreign rule. He was not happy that his country was under Austrian domination, so he moved to Sweden for a time, introducing audiences to the "new" music of Mendelssohn, Liszt, and Wagner. Liszt was his lifelong friend. When the political conditions in his home country improved, he returned and became the musical leader of the Czechs.

> **tone poem** - descriptive music, a poem in music rather than words, also called a symphonic poem.

The Moldau from *My Country*

Smetana
[51] & [52]

Two streams from mountain forest glades meet 'neath a bough.
They laugh and leap down waterfalls to join the Moldau.
We see a wedding feast, the peasants dance as they sing.
We hear the hunting horns and tower bells as they ring.
Reflected castles, water nymphs and naiads at play,
We'll visit Prague and Smetana; this is a perfect day!
The Moldau, Czech river! The Moldau, great river!
       Great river, great river………..

JOHANN STRAUSS, JR.
(1825 - 1899)

Johann (YO-hann) Strauss, Jr. was called the "Waltz King." He couldn't dance a waltz, but he certainly could compose one. The waltz was the popular dance of the nineteenth century in Europe, and the Strausses were the favorite composers of the **genre**. Johann's father was a musician and composer, as were two of his brothers. However, Johann, Jr. is the most famous. His talent was recognized early, and his first composition was published when he was only six! ***The Blue Danube*** is the best-known Strauss waltz, but many of the others are equally delightful. A recording of his waltzes is sure to please. Unlike a symphony, it does not require your full attention and is great for background music.

Johann, Jr. was like a pop star of today. Women proposed to him or tried to get a lock of his hair. Strauss was loved all over Europe, but especially in his own Austria. When his health began to fail, people waited anxiously for news about him. On June 3, 1899, a large crowd had gathered at an outdoor concert. In the middle of the performance, a messenger rushed onto the stage and whispered in the conductor's ear. The conductor stopped the orchestra, and they began to play the *Blue Danube Waltz*. The audience knew immediately that Johann had died. They rose to their feet and bowed their heads. Women cried. His obituary referred to him as "the last symbol of cheerful, pleasant times."

Strauss also wrote operettas, the most popular being ***Die Fledermaus*** (the bat, known in German as the flying mouse). Unlike operas where all dialogue is sung, an ***operetta*** has some spoken dialogue in addition to the solos and chorus.

Die Fledermaus is a romantic comedy in three acts. The story tells about two "friends" who went to a masquerade party. One (Dr. Falke) was dressed in a bat costume. He drank entirely too much at the party and his friend, Eisenstein, let him find his own way home through the streets of the town in his ridiculous costume. When Dr. Falke sobered up, he was not amused that Eisenstein had deserted him.

Die Fledermaus is the story of how Dr. Falke gets even with Eisenstein for leaving him in his bat costume in the streets alone. It is lighthearted and humorous with delightful music by Strauss.

> **genre** - (ZHAHN-rah) distinctive type or category of artistic work

Waltz from *Die Fledermaus*   **Strauss**
[53] & [54]

Knock, knock, knock,
Who do I hear knocking,
Knocking at my door?

    This is Fledermausy,
    Mausy, maus, maus,
    Going to the ball with
    Straussy, Strauss, Strauss.

Who is Fledermausy
Knocking at my housey?
He looks like a bat!

    Ha, ha, ha, ha, ha, ha
    You are right dear,
    Flying mouse, a little bat!

Come to the ball,
To the masquerade,
Come to the ball,
Don't you be afraid.

Come, let us dance,
You will be surprised,
When I remove
This great disguise!

JOHANNES BRAHMS
(1833 - 1897)

Johannes Brahms had an unhappy childhood. His family lived in poverty in a crowded tenement on the waterfront of Hamburg, Germany. His parents fought continuously. Little Johannes hated school, and he often went to bed hungry. However, he loved music. He made up little melodies and wrote them on paper with a kind of musical notation that he had created.

Father Brahms was an amateur musician. He took note of his son's talent and found a piano teacher for him. Johannes learned so quickly that he was soon earning some badly-needed coins by playing in taverns along the waterfront.

Fortunately, when Brahms was ten years old, he was able to take lessons from the best piano teacher in Hamburg. His progress was so rapid that he gave a piano recital when he was only fourteen. He played one of his own compositions.

When Brahms was twenty, a famous violinist asked Johannes to tour with him as his accompanist. This opened many doors for him, since he met many other famous musicians. Liszt praised him, and Robert and Clara Schumann recognized his genius. The Schumanns were lifelong friends with Brahms and helped his music to become known and published.

Like many musicians of the Romantic Period, Brahms moved to Vienna. He wrote four symphonies, one violin concerto, two piano concertos, and the "Double Concerto" for violin, cello and orchestra. He composed in all forms except opera.

It took four years for Brahms to complete his **Symphony No. 1**. It was a great success. One musician called it "Beethoven's Tenth Symphony." Many others called Brahms "Beethoven's heir" because Brahms was seen as the greatest symphonic composer since Beethoven.

We will learn the first theme from the last movement, the Finale (Fi-NALL-ee). A finale is the last part of a composition. (Think of "final.") Great music is truly a gift that keeps giving.

Unlike Beethoven, Brahms became rich from the sales of his compositions. More importantly, he was beloved and acclaimed.

Symphony No. 1, Movement 4 — **Brahms** [55] & [56]

Brahms' First Symphony
Has a melody made for singing.
Brahms' First Symphony
Is a gift he's forever bringing.

    His music is sunshine,
    It's a sure sign
    We'll see flowers blooming.
    Fly butterfly, rainbow high,
    Pure blue sky---
    Come fly on the wings of the wind.

        Brahms' first Symphony
        Has a melody made for singing.
        Brahms' First Symphony
        Is a gift he's forever bringing.

ALMICARE PONCHIELLI
(1834 - 1886)

Almicare Ponchielle (Pon-chee-EL-ee) was an Italian organist and composer who lived in Italy during Verdi's lifetime. Both men composed operas but Ponchielli has only one that has survived in the modern opera **repertoire**. Verdi has twenty-eight operas that are still performed.

The *Dance of the Hours* is a classic ballet which was written for Ponchielli's opera, *La Gioconda.* Ballets are pantomimes which tell a story with music and dance. Many operas include ballets that add spectacular costumes and dancing to the drama.

The opera takes place in Venice. La Gioconda is a beautiful street singer. A spy named Barnaba loves her, but she loves Enzo, a nobleman. However, Enzo loves Laura who is already married to someone else. Doesn't that sound like a modern-day soap opera?

In Act III of the opera, the great hall of the palace is filled with guests. The evening entertainment is a ballet in which the dancers are costumed as the Hours of Dawn, Day, Evening, and Night. They portray the struggle between day and night. In the **finale** the hours of light conquer the hours of darkness. You can see why the music is called *Dance of the Hours*.

You may have heard a funny camp song written to the *Dance of the Hours* music. However, most people don't know the name of the composer who wrote the music. I hope you'll remember it after you've sung the theme a few times. Some children that I know now call corn chips "Ponchielli Chips"!

---

repertoire - (REP-uh-twar) the complete list of operas, dramas, or musical works available for performance
finale - (fi-NALL-ee) the final part of a musical work

Dance of the Hours - from *La Gioconda* **Ponchielli [57] & [58]**

Ponchielli, watching telly,
Eating corn chips, filling belly,
Watching ballet, Dance of Hours,
Dawn and daytime,
Evening, night time,
It's the right time.

        Ponchielli, tired of telly,
        Eating too much, aching belly.
        Couch potato, better move it,
            Why not groove it!
            Dance ballet
            Live right.

PETER ILYICH TCHAIKOVSKY
(1840-1893)

Peter Ilyich Tchaikovsky (chai-KOV-skee), probably the most famous Russian composer, wrote ballets, symphonies, overtures, concertos, and operas. His music was not nationalistic enough for the "**Russian Five**"* to include him in that group. He was a true romantic composer, showing great emotion, sensitivity and warmth in his music. You can find two of Tchaikovsky's ballets, *Swan Lake* and *The Nutcracker Suite,* in *Themes To Remember* **Volume 1** and **2**. Now you can learn a theme from Tchaikovsky's *Sleeping Beauty* ballet in this volume.

Tchaikovsky did not devote himself totally to music until he was twenty-two. His parents sent him away to school when he was only ten. They arranged for him to be trained as a lawyer, but he was unhappy in that profession. He found comfort in music, and he started to educate himself and to compose. He quit his job at the Ministry of Justice and attended a music school that later became the St. Petersburg Conservatory. He taught for a while, but his love was composition.

A rich widow, Madame von Meck, gave Tchaikovsky an allowance for life that allowed him to compose music full time. They wrote to each other regularly for thirteen years, but they never met. Madame von Meck had told Tchaikovsky that he must make no attempt to meet her personally, or the money and friendship would end. Wouldn't it be nice if every composer could find a Madame von Meck?

Tchaikovsky composed two piano concertos, but **Concerto No. 1** is the best known. The theme from the first movement was used for a popular song called *Tonight We Love.* Tchaikovsky also composed one violin concerto, which is a "must-have" for your music library.

Romeo and Juliet is a fantasy-overture. Some **overtures** are meant as an introduction to an opera, oratorio or similar work. Other overtures, such as *Romeo and Juliet,* stand by themselves. (See Glossary, p.109.) In this fantasy-overture, Tchaikovsky creates a mood that captures the tragedy of Shakespeare's play.

Tchaikovsky's ballets are works that combine music and drama with a dignity and beauty that had not been reached before his time. His symphonies, concertos, overtures, and ballets continue to enrich the world.

*Balakirev (Bah-LAH-ke-ref), Cui (kwee), Borodin, Mussorgsky, and Rimsky-Korsakov

Piano Concerto No. 1, Mvt. 1

Tchaikovsky
[59] & [60]

Concerto One - Yeah!
Tchaikovsky Two - Yeah!
Piano Three, get set,
Let's go now,
Now, two three, one two,
Tonight we sing songs of love,
Beneath the moon and the stars.
Tonight we pray God above
Will bless our love
And guide our stars.
Tonight we sing our song of love
'Neath the moon, Ah……….

Sleeping Beauty — **Tchaikovsky [61] & [62]**

Act 1: In an ancient kingdom, the Princess Aurora's birth is being celebrated. The King and Queen have consulted with the Chamberlain to make sure that every important guest has been invited including the Fairy Godmothers. But somehow the oldest and most powerful fairy, the wicked Carabosse, was left off the list. Although the Fairies plead with her not to be angry at the King and Queen, Carabosse predicts that the princess will prick her finger on a spindle and die on her sixteenth birthday. But the good Lilac Fairy has power to change the curse. She says the princess will not die. Instead, she and the entire kingdom will fall into a long, deep sleep until the day when a handsome prince awakens her with a kiss.

Act 2, Scene 1: The kingdom is celebrating Aurora's birthday when a mysterious old woman offers a bouquet of flowers to the princess. Aurora pricks her finger on the spindle hidden inside the bouquet, and she falls lifeless to the ground. Carabosse triumphantly throws off her cape. Her prediction has come true! But hope returns as the Lilac Fairy appears and calmly tells everyone that their long sleep is about to begin with the Fairy Godmothers standing guard.

Act 2, Scene 2: One hundred years later a prince is wandering in the forest. The forest fairies lead him to the Lilac Fairy who asks him why he is so sad. He tells her he has no true love. The Lilac Fairy shows him a vision of Aurora and offers to lead him to the sleeping princess.

Act 3: The Lilac Fairy leads him to the mysterious castle where he kisses Aurora and awakens the entire kingdom! Good has triumphed over evil and the court rejoices. Everyone celebrates the upcoming wedding.

Sleeping Beauty

Tchaikovsky
[61] & [62]

Sleeping Beauty,
Who cast the spell that made you sleep?
Sleeping Beauty,
Here comes the Prince so don't you weep,
For he'll kiss you and
Then Tchaikovsky has plans for you
To dance ballet!

77

Shakespeare's *Romeo and Juliet*   Tchaikovsky [63] & [64]

The Montagues (MON-tuh-gews, Romeo's family) and Capulets (Cap-u-LETS, Juliet's family) have been fighting for many years, but Romeo and Juliet meet and instantly fall in love. Romeo goes to her house and finds Juliet on her balcony. They promise to love each other forever! They arrange to meet at Friar Laurence's place where they are secretly married.

But the two families begin to fight again. In a street scene Juliet's cousin, Tybalt, kills Romeo's friend, Mercutio. Then Romeo kills Tybalt. The Duke of Verona banishes Romeo from the city. Before he leaves, Romeo and Juliet enjoy one night of love.

Juliet's father, not knowing that Juliet is married to Romeo, insists that she is to marry Paris, a handsome and wealthy suitor. Juliet goes to Friar Laurence for advice. He gives her a small flask of sleeping potion that makes her appear dead. Her family has a funeral instead of a wedding for Juliet. They place her in a tomb. The Friar sends a letter to Romeo telling him what has happened. He tells Romeo to come get Juliet and together they can escape from the city.

Before that letter reaches him, Romeo hears by word of mouth that Juliet has died. He buys some poison and goes to the tomb of his bride. He finds Paris there. Paris thinks Romeo is a grave robber, and he draws his sword. Romeo is desperate and, in the fight, he kills Paris. Then he kisses Juliet and drinks the poison. When Juliet wakes, she sees that Romeo is dead. She seizes his dagger and plunges it into her heart.

The friar tells the families what has happened to Romeo and Juliet. The story of their tender and beautiful love shames the two families, and they promise to end the feud of many years.

Leonard Bernstein - a modern pianist, composer, conductor - used the Romeo and Juliet plot for his musical theater work, *West Side Story.*

(To help you keep the families straight, remember that Capulet rhymes with Juliet.)

Romeo and Juliet

Tchaikovsky
[63] & [64]

Romeo, come find your Juliet,
She lies sleeping, this lovely Capulet.
As Shakespeare told your tale,
Tchaikovsky sings it, too.
You're much too young to die,
We have to question why.

Young lovers killed by hate,
A tragedy of fate
That only love can break.
Romeo, come find your Juliet.
She lies sleeping,
This lovely Capulet.

QUESTIONS FOR THE MUSICAL PRODIGY - ROMANTIC PERIOD

	Page
1. Forte wears a hat like which Romantic Period American president?	46
2. Richard Wagner is best known for what kind of compositions?	54
3. Who wrote *Aïda*, *Nabucco* and *Rigoletto*?	56
4. The Romantic Period composers composed primarily for whom?	47
5. Which composer was famous for comic operas that made people laugh?	62
6. Was Juliet a Montague or a Capulet?	78
7. What is a *Fledermaus*?	68
8. Through which city does the Moldau River flow?	66
9. Who likes to eat corn chips and watch telly?	73
10. Who were the two Czech composers who used folk songs in their music?	66
11. Who wrote a gigantic opera based on German and Norse mythology?	54
12. How did Romantic Period composers make a living?	47
13. Who introduced Bach's forgotten music to the world?	48
14. Whose operas used a distinctive theme (*Leitmotif*) for each character?	54
15. Who wrote an opera which takes place in Egypt?	56
16. What is an opera?	56
17. What is an operetta?	62
18. What is a libretto?	56
19. Who was known as "Mr. Opera"?	56
20. Which composer had a French father and a Polish mother?	50
21. Who built his own opera house for the *Ring of the Nibelungs?*.	54
22. Who looked back and lost his wife Eurydice?	64
23. Who wrote an opera about the exile of the Jews to Babylon?	56
24. The Valkyries were the daughters of whom?	55
25. In opera, what is recitative singing?	56
26. What does the French word *tristesse* mean?	52
27. In an opera, what kind of music is an aria?	56
28. Who wrote *Songs Without Words* including the *Spring Song*?	48
29. Who was the brilliant pianist who wrote beautiful melodies?	50
30. What is a virtuoso?	50
31. The story of *Orpheus and Eurydice* comes from which mythology?	64
32. What is an étude?	50
33. Who wrote the play about *Romeo and Juliet?*	74
34. Who wrote the ballet about *Romeo and Juliet?*	74
35. What is a tone poem (also called a symphonic poem)?	66
36. Which composer was lucky enough to be supported by a rich widow?	74
37. Which birds died dancing the *Can Can*?	63

To think about: Three composers had parents who persuaded them to study for careers other than music. (p. 16, 42, & 74). Was this a good idea?

Good Listening from the Romantic Period

Mendelssohn
   Violin Concerto in E minor
   Capriccio Brillant

Chopin
   Waltzes, Nocturnes, and Preludes
   Tristesse Étude
   Fantasie-Impromptu

Brahms
   Piano Quintet in F minor
   Waltzes and Cello Sonatas
   Symphony No. 1

Liszt
   Hungarian Rhapsodies No. 1 - 15
   Les Préludes

Verdi
   Aïda: Gloria all' Egitto (Act 2)
   Nabucco: "Va, pensiero" (Chorus of Hebrew Slaves)

Offenbach
   Orpheus in the Underworld - Overture
   Tales of Hoffman

Smetana
   Quartet No. 1 in E minor

Dvořák
   String Quartet in F (*American*)
   Slavonic Dances
   Concerto in B minor, Op. 104, Cello and Orchestra

Johann Strauss
   Waltzes
   Overture, *Die Fledermaus*

Mussorgsky
   Pictures at an Exhibition

Grieg
   Piano Concerto in A minor
   Peer Gynt Suites No. 1 and No. 2

Tchaikovsky
   Violin Concerto in D
   Piano Concerto No. 1 in B Flat minor
   Sleeping Beauty
   Romeo and Juliet
   Symphony No. 6, *Pathétique*

MODERN

Piano and Forte Go Modern

(1900 to the Present)

Piano and Forte Relaxing the Rules

THE MODERN PERIOD   (1900 to the Present)

DEBUSSY, Claude	(1862 - 1918)
SATIE, Erik	(1866 - 1925)
JOPLIN, Scott	(1869 - 1917)
STRAVINSKY, Igor	(1882 - 1971)
PROKOFIEV, Serge	(1891 - 1953)

During each period composers try to express themselves in new ways. They break the rules of the previous period and try new forms, harmonies, and rhythms. In the **Modern Period**, composers experimented more than in most periods. For instance, Twentieth Century music includes jazz, rock and roll, electronic music, whole-tone and twelve-tone scale music, computer music, and "chance" music.

Why do composers want to experiment? They want to find new ways to express their ideas. A good composer will write high quality music reflecting the times in which he lives. He will express the human experience of his time. If he succeeds, his music will endure. If the work has no depth, like some popular music, it will likely be forgotten.

Modern music uses a lot more **dissonance** than earlier music. A dissonant sound is one that clashes, that may sound "wrong" to our ears. In modern music we have become quite accustomed to dissonant sounds in music. Prokofiev's March from *The Love for Three Oranges* is delightfully dissonant.

Modern composers also use rhythms that are more jagged and **syncopated** and meters that change from bar to bar. Scott Joplin's piano rags make continuous use of syncopation. Syncopated music accents the weak beats. It is hard to sit still when you hear it.

Stravinsky's ballet, *The Rite of Spring,* caused a riot in the theater at its first performance. The people thought it was brutal primitivism and not suited for the concert hall. The **Infernal Dance** in **Volume 1** of *Themes To Remember* is also extremely syncopated and dissonant. But even adults gradually adjust to new sounds in music and begin to accept them as normal. Stravinsky's *Petrouchka* also incorporates vivid polytonality and asymmetrical rhythms but not in the theme that we sing in this volume. It is a sad song about a sad little puppet!

While many composers press forward with new ideas, others cling to the past and present. It has always been so, but we continue to accept the new while keeping the best of the past.

> **dissonant** - a sound that clashes, which may sound "wrong" to our ears
> **syncopated** - music in which the weak beats are accented - jazzy

CLAUDE DEBUSSY
(1862 - 1918)

Claude DEBUSSY (duh-bu-SEE) from France is said to have started the **Modern Period** with his impressionist style. He created beauty with impressions rather than with clear images. His melodies evoke dreamy, misty feelings, like looking at a scene through a fog or in the moonlight. He painted pictures with sound. If possible, listen to all of *Clair de lune* or *Reverie* while you look at a Monet painting. You will understand Impressionism better by listening and looking than by reading.

Debussy was a wonderful pianist who wrote most of his music for the piano. He was known as a musical rebel. He irritated his teachers with the new sounds he produced. He searched for new chords and new scales; he initiated the **whole-tone scale**. If you have a piano, start on any key and play every other key (don't forget the black keys) until you decide to stop. You will see how Debussy produced a harp-like sound of misty, moonlight magic. He flunked his music composition course! His teachers certainly didn't expect him to become a famous composer.

In 1889, Debussy attended the World's Fair in Paris. The Eiffel Tower was built for this fair, and many countries participated in art and music displays. Debussy was fascinated by the subtle paintings and elaborately decorated vases from Japan. He was also intrigued by the exotic sounds of the Javanese gamelan, an orchestra of flutes, strings and delicately toned percussion instruments that are shaped something like flower pots. Javanese gamelan orchestras play complicated rhythms with a shimmering, ethereal sound.

Debussy used irregular rhythms, unusual chord progressions and whole-tone scales to create dreamy music. *Reverie* means "dream" in French.

---

whole-tone scale - a scale which has a whole step between each tone. It has neither a tonic (I), nor a dominant (V), nor a leading tone (VII). The lack of a key center gives the scale a feeling of vagueness and restlessness. Debussy adopted it as a suitable vocabulary for **Impressionism** in music.

Reverie **Debussy [65] & [66]**

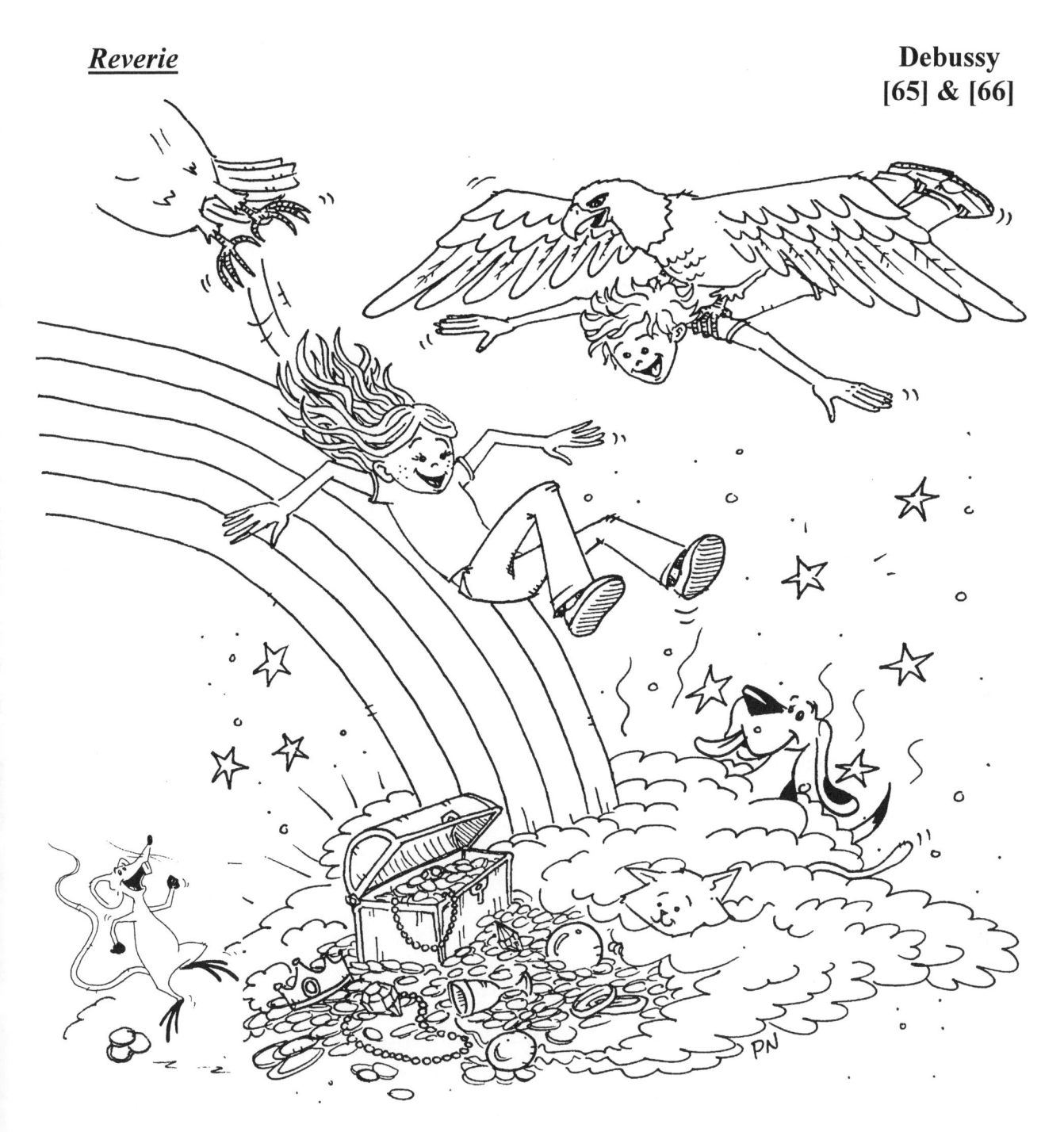

Debussy Reverie, Debussy Reverie,
Dreaming, Debussy Reverie
I dream, too,
Dream that I can fly with you.

    Flying, like an eagle we're gliding,
    Down a rainbow we're sliding,
    At the end of the rainbow
    We'll find many treasures!

ERIK SATIE
(1866 - 1925)

Erik Satie (Sah-TEE) was a French composer whose music had more influence on other composers than on audiences. He wanted to free French music from German influence. He said, "We want our own music---without kraut."

Satie was noted for his jokes and unconventional behavior. He gave his compositions strange titles and wrote funny directions and explanations throughout his music. One of his titles was, "Three Pieces in the Form of a Pear." Some of his strange directions were, "Light as an egg," and "Like a nightingale with a toothache." To get sounds of modern life, he introduced into his orchestra a typewriter, an airplane engine, and other noisemakers.

There are three *Gymnopédies* (zshim-noh-pay-dees) but we will learn only the theme for No. 1. The long melodic lines pull against simple chords. The Gymnopédies suggest the slow athletic dances of ancient Greece. Instead of major and minor scales, Satie used scales more like those of ancient music.

Satie became the leader of the young rebels in the arts. He also influenced younger composers such as Aaron Copland and John Cage. He taught composers that music does not have to shout or beat the drum to be heard. He taught the art of simplicity.

Not all of Satie's music is witty. He wrote the beautiful *Messe des pauvres* (*Mass For the Poor*) for the working-class people of his hometown. One of his last works was *Socrate,* which he called a "symphonic drama." It tells the story of the death of Socrates in quiet music for voices and a chamber orchestra. The music never rises to a climax. It is as simple as Plato's report of Socrates' death.

(Socrates lived in Greece from 469-399 B.C. He taught young people to think, but the rulers were afraid of new ideas so they condemned him to die. He refused to escape and drank poison hemlock with noble calm and courage. He wrote nothing, but his pupil, Plato, wrote about him.)

Gymnopédie　　　　　　　　　　　　　　　　　　　　　　　　　　**Satie**
　　　　　　　　　　　　　　　　　　　　　　　　　　　　　　　　[67] & [68]

Gymnopédie by Erik Satie,
　　Ooooo
　　　　Gymnopédie, tears fall down
　　　　　　Like rain,
　　　　　　　　Soothing rain.
　　　　　　　　　　Tears heal my pain,
　　　　　　　　　I can love once again.
　　　　　　　　　　Ooooo..........
　　　　　　　　　　　　I love you, Ooooo

SCOTT JOPLIN
(1869- 1917)

Scott Joplin is the most famous **ragtime** composer and pianist. ***The Entertainer*** is his best known composition. It was made popular by a movie in the 1970's called *The Sting,* starring Paul Newman and Robert Redford.

Born in Texas, Scott Joplin grew up in a large musical family. His father, a former slave, had been a plantation fiddler, his mother a singer. Scott learned to play several instruments and taught himself to play the piano. An old German music teacher heard of Joplin's talents. He was so impressed that he gave Scott free piano and harmony lessons. He taught Joplin about the works of the great European masters. In his early teens Joplin sang, played and taught professionally. He organized a touring vocal group. He moved to St. Louis where he played piano in clubs, cafes, and **honky-tonks**. He also toured a **vaudeville** circuit singing in his own eight-voice double quartet.

At George R. Smith College in Missouri, Joplin studied music and worked seriously at composition. He developed his own piano style of **ragtime** music. Ragtime music has a strong syncopation in the melody with a regularly accented accompaniment. Ragtime was, for a while, the name for any kind of jazz. Classical melodies were even given the ragtime treatment in a style known as "ragging the classics." The earliest jazz bands in New Orleans were called "ragtime bands." Ragtime music was popular on player pianos, in early movies, and in the old-time saloons. American ragtime became popular in Europe. Stravinsky wrote *Ragtime* for eleven instruments (1918) and *Piano Rag-Music* (1920).

The *Maple Leaf Rag* was Joplin's first big success. It was named after a dance hall where he had taught and played. The *Maple Leaf Rag* sold hundreds of thousands of copies and brought fame to both Scott and his publisher. It also brought financial security. Joplin was greatly encouraged and began producing many piano rags, marches, and waltzes. He also tried his hand at ballet and opera but his fame rests on his ragtime music. It has become a part of "classical" American music.

---

ragtime - a style of piano jazz that was played in honky-tonk cafés in the 1890's.
honky-tonk - a cheap, noisy, garish nightclub or dance hall
vaudeville - a light, often comic, theatrical show combining pantomime, dialogue, dancing, and song -- may include acrobats, comedians, and performing animals

The Entertainer

Joplin
[69] & [70]

Ragtime's the way to go,
Joplin's the guy to know.
Now is the time
To start the show.   Yeah!

(Boy)
Let's dance ragtime, let's syncopate,
Razamataz, I love jazz, it's first rate!
Let's dance ragtime, let's celebrate,
Joplin's honky-tonk jazz
We'll demonstrate!

(Girl)
Mom says I can't stay out too late!
And Dad says, "Better be home before eight."
Mom says, "It's your first date."
And Dad says, "Don't osculate."
And Mom says, "Don't tolerate holding hands."

Spoken: But -----How can we dance?

osculate - to kiss

89

IGOR STRAVINSKY
(1882 - 1971)

Igor Stravinsky (struh-VIN-skee) was born in Russia near St. Petersburg. He influenced his contemporaries more than any other composer of the Modern Period. He wrote in many styles and forms: opera, ballet, symphony orchestra, church, and player piano. He wrote *Circus Polka* for the elephants in the Ringling Brothers' Circus and *Ebony Concerto* for Woody Herman's dance band. His music has heavy rhythms with irregular and changing meters. No matter what he wrote in which style, one could always tell that it was by Stravinsky.

Stravinsky's father was a leading bass singer in the Russian Imperial Opera. Igor began studying piano at the age of nine, but preferred to improvise or read his father's opera scores instead of practicing his lessons. He attended the university to study law, and there he met Rimsky-Korsakov, the father of a classmate. Rimsky-Korsakov recognized Igor's talent and offered to teach him composition and orchestration.

In 1906 Stravinsky got married and wrote his first successful ballet, *The Firebird*. Soon after, he wrote *The Rite of Spring* and also **Petrushka** (Puh-TROOSH-kuh), the sad story of a puppet. All three ballets drew on Russian folklore and folk tunes. His complex rhythms and **dissonant** sounds shocked people of that time. The primitive rhythms and harsh sounds of *The Rite of Spring* caused a riot in the theater at the first performance. The subtitle reads, "Scenes of Pagan Russia." Stravinsky described it as a solemn pagan rite, with sage elders seated in a circle watching a young girl dance herself to death. They were sacrificing her to please the god of Spring. Stravinsky was clearly the most adventuresome composer of his day. He was perhaps the most influential composer of the twentieth century. Whether composers accepted his ideas or rejected them, they always considered them.

To avoid the Russian Revolution, Stravinsky moved to Switzerland in 1917. From there he moved to France and became a citizen. Both his wife and mother died in 1939. He remarried, moved to Hollywood, and became a citizen of the United States. He was very popular and toured both Europe and the United States, playing his compositions. He died in New York in 1971.

> **dissonant** - a sound that clashes, which may sound "wrong" to our ears

Petrouchka - **The Story of the Ballet**

Stravinsky [71] & [72]

Petrouchka is a sad little puppet with a heart and soul. He longs to know that someone loves him, but he is owned by a mysterious magician who loves no one. If only he could catch a snowflake on his tongue, run and play, or smell a flower, he knows he would be happy. But the magician controls him with the melody he plays on his flute, so Petrouchka is not allowed freedom to live his life as he wishes.

Each year the magician brings his three puppets to the St. Petersburg Fair. Everyone waits eagerly for them to perform. The magician plays a haunting melody on his flute, and suddenly the three life-size puppets come from their booths and begin to dance. First, a lovely ballerina charms the crowds. Then an imposing Moor, and finally the clumsy, sad little clown named Petrouchka appears. As the puppets dance, people begin to notice that they have no strings attached and that they seem almost human.

The ballerina dances a lovely, graceful dance. The Moor, with **scimitar** at his side, is bold and proud. The crowd is fascinated by his powerful dancing. Petrouchka, however, dances clumsily in his ridiculous clown suit and the people laugh at him. He feels like crying. If people only knew that their laughing hurts his heart. He wishes he could cry.

---

scimitar - a short saber with a curved blade

91

Petrouchka

Stravinsky [71] & [72]

Petrouchka loves the ballerina, but she thinks he is strange and awkward. She likes the Moor much better. Petrouchka is very jealous when the ballerina dances with the Moor. He picks up a stick from the ground and shakes it at the Moor. The Moor is not frightened by the sorry little clown, and Petrouchka starts to run away. He falls and the Moor pins him to the ground with his foot. The crowd gasps. Are these puppets or real people?

The magician orders them all to their tents. Petrouchka is miserable. He imagines the ballerina with the Moor and becomes desperate to save her. Finally he finds a way to slip out of his tent. He makes his way to the Moor's tent and sees the ballerina sitting on the Moor's lap. Petrouchka is furious. He bursts into the Moor's tent and shakes his fist at him. At first the Moor is only scornful, but he becomes angry and draws his huge scimitar. Petrouchka runs but the Moor chases him into the square. As the people watch in horror, the Moor brings his scimitar down on Petrouchka and kills him.

The people call the police, but the magician says that Petrouchka is only a puppet and asks why are they making such a fuss. He drags Petrouchka's limp body back toward the booth. Then the magician hears music, the tune that he had played for Petrouchka to dance. He looks up and sees Petrouchka himself standing on the top of the booth. This is the real Petrouchka who is now free to love, to smell the flowers, and to catch snowflakes on his tongue.

babushka - buh-BOOSH-kuh - a Russian grandmother

Petrouchka

Stravinsky
[71] & [72]

Poor Petrouchka, don't you cry.
They wouldn't laugh if they knew why.
Your love is lost, your ballerina.
Love and joy will find you by and by.

    Poor Petrouchka, don't you cry.
    You'll catch a snowflake if you try.
    Go with **Babushka**, catch a star, and
    You'll find heaven where you are.

SERGEI PROKOFIEV
(1891 - 1953)

Sergei Prokofiev (Pro-KO-fee-ev) was one of Russia's greatest composers. His mother taught him to play the piano and encouraged him to make up his own pieces. By the age of nine he had written a three-act opera. He studied music and composition with Rimsky-Korsakov.

Prokofiev wrote all types of compositions: operas, ballets, concertos, symphonies, quartets, music for films, marches, songs and much more. *Peter and the Wolf* is one of his best known works.

During the Russian Revolution in 1918, Prokofiev left Russia. He visited Japan and lived in the United States and Paris for a while. For the Chicago Opera Company he wrote an opera, ***The Love for Three Oranges***. It is a comedy mocking the various tastes of different audiences. It is also a **play-within-a-play.**

In 1933, after fifteen years away from Russia, Prokofiev went home. Musicians, as well as government officials, welcomed him with open arms. He became one of his country's most honored and highly praised men.

Prokofiev was one of the great masters of the orchestra. He varied his music from massive orchestral sounds to simple flute and clarinet duets. His music is always clear, often a simple melody with an interesting accompaniment. His harmony is sometimes dissonant and surprising to the ear, with unexpected key changes.

The March from the ***The Love for Three Oranges*** will be one of your favorite classical themes.

---

play-within-a-play - a play about another play. For example, you could be watching a play about some children who are giving a school play for their parents. Some of the children would be the actors on stage and some would be the parents watching the show. All of them would be on the stage.

The Love for Three Oranges - Story of the Opera

Prokofiev
[73] & [74]

Prince Tartaglia is incurably sick. The doctors say that he can perhaps be cured if he can be made to laugh. Various people in the court try to make the Prince laugh but to no avail. The Prince also has enemies in the court who would like to see him die so they can take over the throne. Fata Morgana, a witch, comes to aid the enemies. She says that nobody will be able to laugh while she is present. However, she struggles with the jester to get near the prince and flips in the air doing a somersault. This is so funny that the Prince begins to laugh and laugh, just the opposite of what the witch had planned.

This makes the witch angry, so she turns to the Prince and puts a spell upon him. He is condemned to fall in love with **Three Oranges** who are far away. He will feel that he must find them at all costs. So he sets out with his friend, Truffaldino**,** on the long and dangerous quest to find the Three Oranges.

95

The Love for Three Oranges   **Prokofiev**
[73] & [74]

The Prince and Truffaldino next find themselves in a desert. A good magician tells them that they will find the Three Oranges held by a wicked magician who looks like a cook. He is frightful and can kill a man with one blow of his soup ladle. The good magician gives the Prince a magic ribbon to distract the wicked magician while the Prince steals the Three Oranges. The good magician warns the Prince that if he ever gets the Three Oranges, he must cut them open only when near water. Otherwise, the gravest trouble will befall them.

As predicted, the cook is intrigued by the magic ribbon, and while he is busy watching it, the Prince and Truffaldino steal the Three Oranges. Next, we find them out in the desert struggling to carry the Oranges, which have grown to an enormous size, big enough to hold people!

The Prince is sleepy so he puts the Oranges down and goes to sleep. Truffaldino is very thirsty and reasons that the Oranges would be juicy. He takes his sword and splits open an Orange. Out walks a princess. She is also very thirsty and says that she must have water immediately or she will die.

Truffaldino cuts open the second Orange hoping to get juice, but a second princess walks out, just as thirsty as the first! The princesses collapse. Truffaldino cannot stand to see them die, so he goes off into the desert.

The Prince wakes up, sees the two dead princesses and he cuts open the third Orange. Out steps Princess Ninetta. The Prince immediately knows that this is his true love, but she too will die if he doesn't find water immediately. Some of the chorus members in the "play-within-a-play" bring a pail of water to Princess Ninetta and she is saved! After a few more magic spells, she is allowed to marry the Prince. And, of course, they live happily ever after.

The Love for Three Oranges - **March**

**Prokofiev
[73] & [74]**

Alex and Jessalyn DeVine guarding the magic oranges!

Prokofiev needs the oranges for his opera production.

Who's that knocking at my door?
Late at night, what a fright,
Knock no more!
This is no fun!
   CALL 911
We'd better run!
We'd better run!
(1) PROKOFIEV is that you?
(2) Prokofiev, Prokofiev, Prokofiev
   COME RIGHT IN! **(Fine)**

[: He's looking for his oranges
   For his magic oranges!
   Not just one!
   Not just two,
But all three of them! :]
        (D.C. al Fine)

QUESTIONS FOR THE MUSICAL PRODIGIES - MODERN PERIOD

	Page
1. In the Modern Period there are many composition rules.　　T or F	83
2. Who wrote music that sounds like misty moonlight?	84
3. Who wrote funny instructions like "Light as an egg" in his music?	86
4. Who was the most famous composer of ragtime music?	88
5. Which modern composer wrote a ballet that caused a riot in the theater?	90
6. In *Love for Three Oranges,* who brings a pail of water for the princess?	97
7. Modern classical music includes many types of compositions. T or F	83
8. What is a whole-tone scale?	84
9. Who initiated the whole-tone scale?	84
10. Describe Impressionism in music and art.	84
11. What is syncopated music?	(Glossary)
12. What does dissonant mean?	83
13. In which music period would you find the most dissonance?	83
14. In which music period would you find the most syncopation?	83
15. What does the French word *reverie* mean?	84
16. His father was a slave and a plantation fiddler. Who was he?	88
17. Who composed *The Firebird* and *Petrouchka?*	90
18. What does "ragging the classics" mean?	88
19. Who wrote music that is very syncopated and dissonant?	90
20. Who used a typewriter and other noisemakers in his music?	86
21. Whose music used ancient scales and simplicity?	86
22. Which composer wrote about the death of Socrates?	86
23. Who wrote *Circus Polka* for the Ringling Brothers' Circus elephants?	90
24. In Petrouchka, how does the magician control his puppets?	91
25. Why does Petrouchka go after the Moor with a stick?	92
26. What does the Moor do to Petrouchka when he shakes the stick at him?	92
27. What does the Moor do to Petrouchka at the end of the ballet?	92
28. At the end of the ballet, is Petrouchka dead?	92

To think about: Can a puppet die? What do you think the story is telling you?

Good Listening from the Modern Period

Debussy
Prelude to the Afternoon of a Faun
La Mer (The Sea)

Satie
Gymnopédies, No. 1, 2, & 3
Gnossiennes

Joplin
Piano Rags

Stravinsky
L'histoire du soldat (*The Soldier's Tale*)
The Firebird Ballet Suite
Petrouchka

Prokofiev
Peter and the Wolf
Classical Symphony

Rachmaninoff
Piano Concerto No. 2 in A minor
Rhapsody on a Theme of Paganini

Ravel
Boléro
Rhapsodie espagnole

Gershwin
Rhapsody in Blue
American in Paris
Piano Concerto in F

Copland
Clarinet Concerto
Fanfare for the Common Man
Appalachian Spring
Rodeo

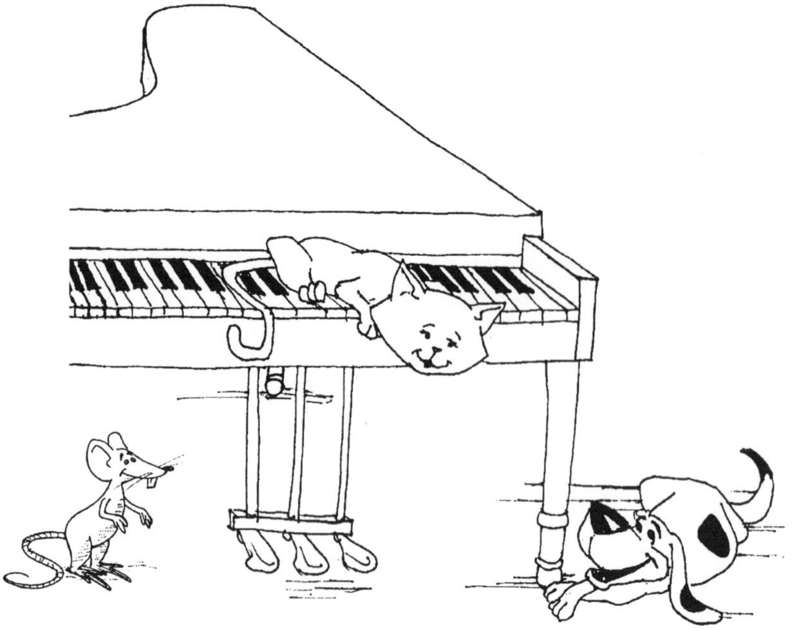

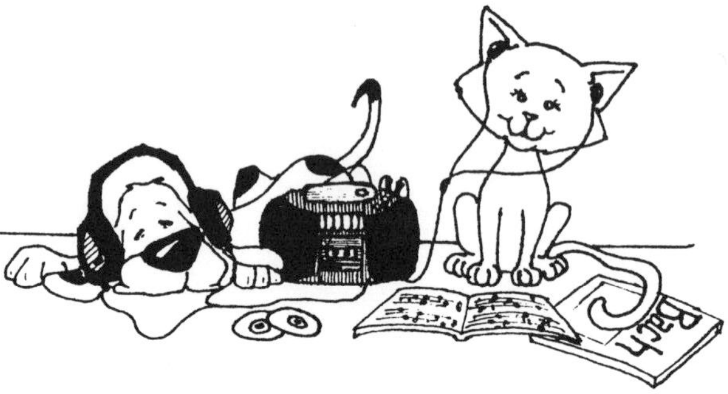
Bach

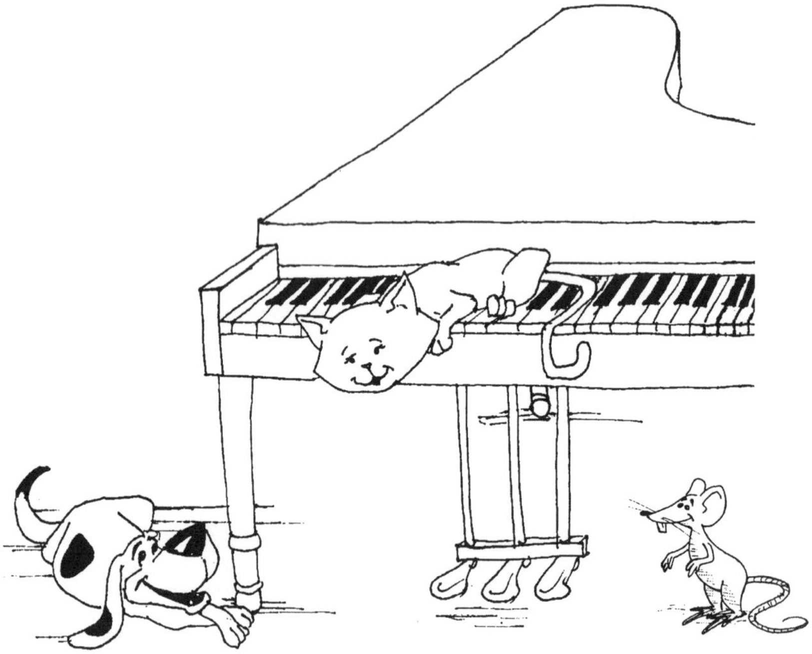

APPENDIX 1---MUSICAL NOTATION

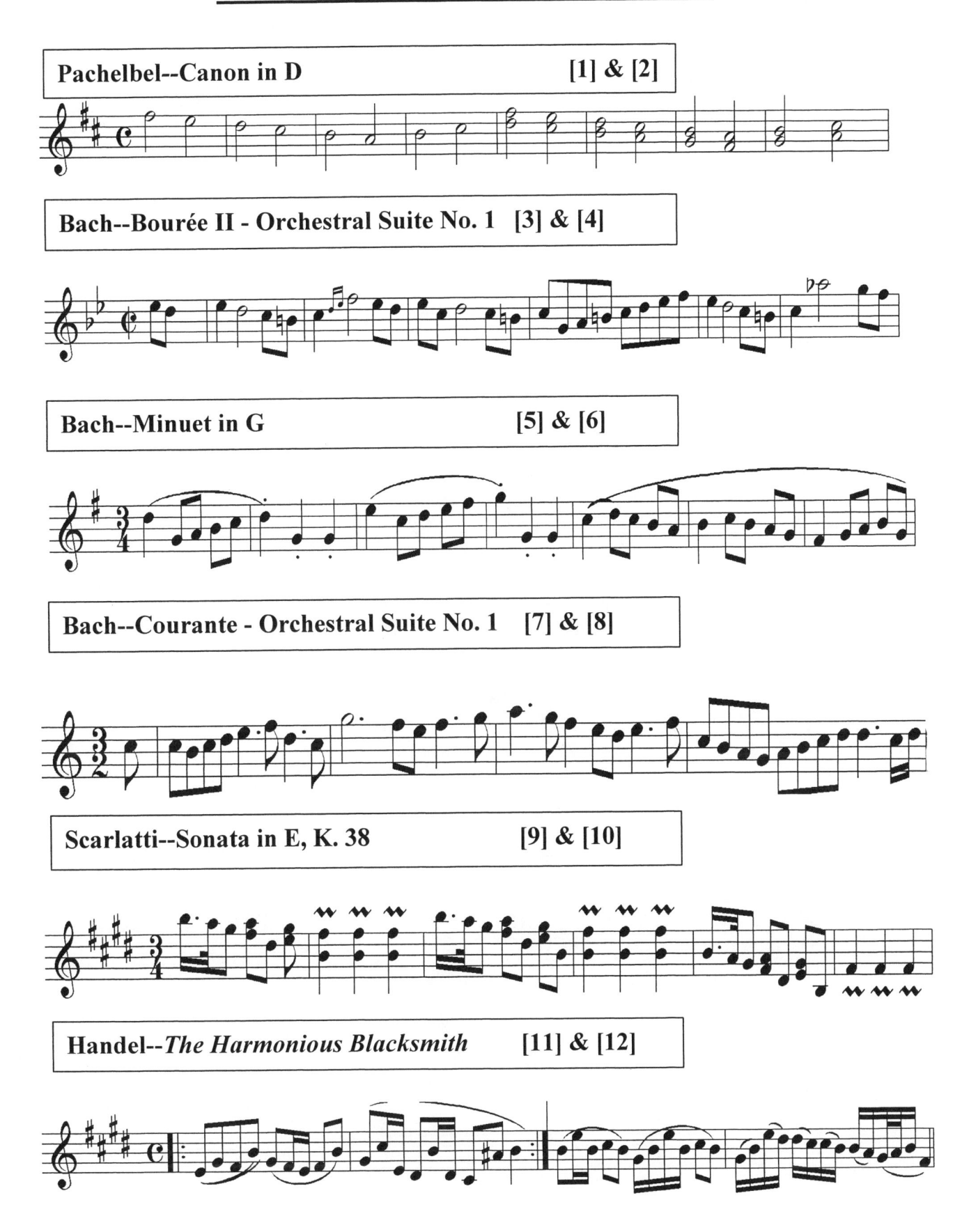

Pachelbel--Canon in D [1] & [2]

Bach--Bourée II - Orchestral Suite No. 1 [3] & [4]

Bach--Minuet in G [5] & [6]

Bach--Courante - Orchestral Suite No. 1 [7] & [8]

Scarlatti--Sonata in E, K. 38 [9] & [10]

Handel--*The Harmonious Blacksmith* [11] & [12]

Haydn--The *Clock* Symphony--Mvt. 1, *Adagio the Cat*   [13] & [14]

Haydn--The *Clock* Symphony--Mvt. 1, *Tickety Tock*   [13] & [14]

Haydn--The *Clock* Symphony--Mvt. 2, *Hear the Clock Tick*   [15] & [16]

Haydn--The *Clock* Symphony--Mvt. 3, *Be Still Little Mouse*   [17] & [18]

Haydn--The *Clock* Symphony--Mvt. 4, *Cat's Going Home*   [19] & [20]

Haydn--The *Drum Roll* Symphony--Mvt. 4   [21] & [22]

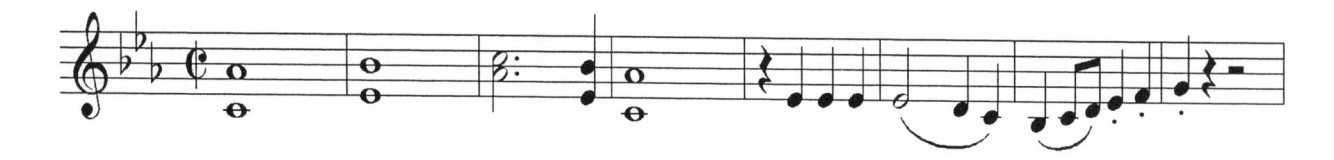

Mozart--Minuet from *Don Juan* [23] & [24]

Mozart--Piano Sonata in C - K. 545 [25] & [26]

Beethoven--*Für Elise* [27] & [28]

Beethoven--*Turkish March* [29] & [30]

Beethoven--Symphony No. 5, Mvt. 4 [31] & [32]

Schubert--Serenade [33] & [34]

Mendelssohn--*Spring Song* [35] & [36]

Chopin--*Fantasie-Impromptu* [37] & [38]

Chopin--*Tristesse* Étude [39] & [40]

Wagner--*Ride of the Valkyries* [41] & [42]

Verdi--*Nabucco* - Overture [43] & [44]

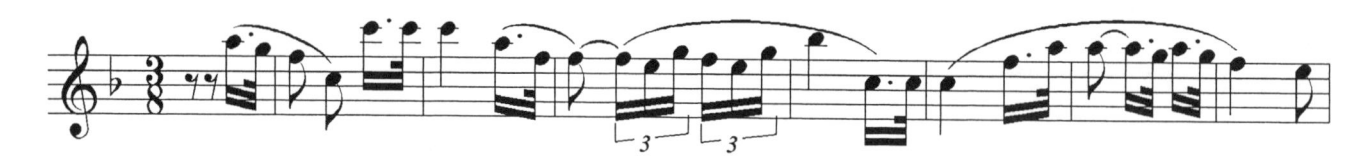

Verdi--*Triumphal March* from *Aïda* [45] & [46]

Offenbach--*Orpheus in the Underworld* [47] & [48]

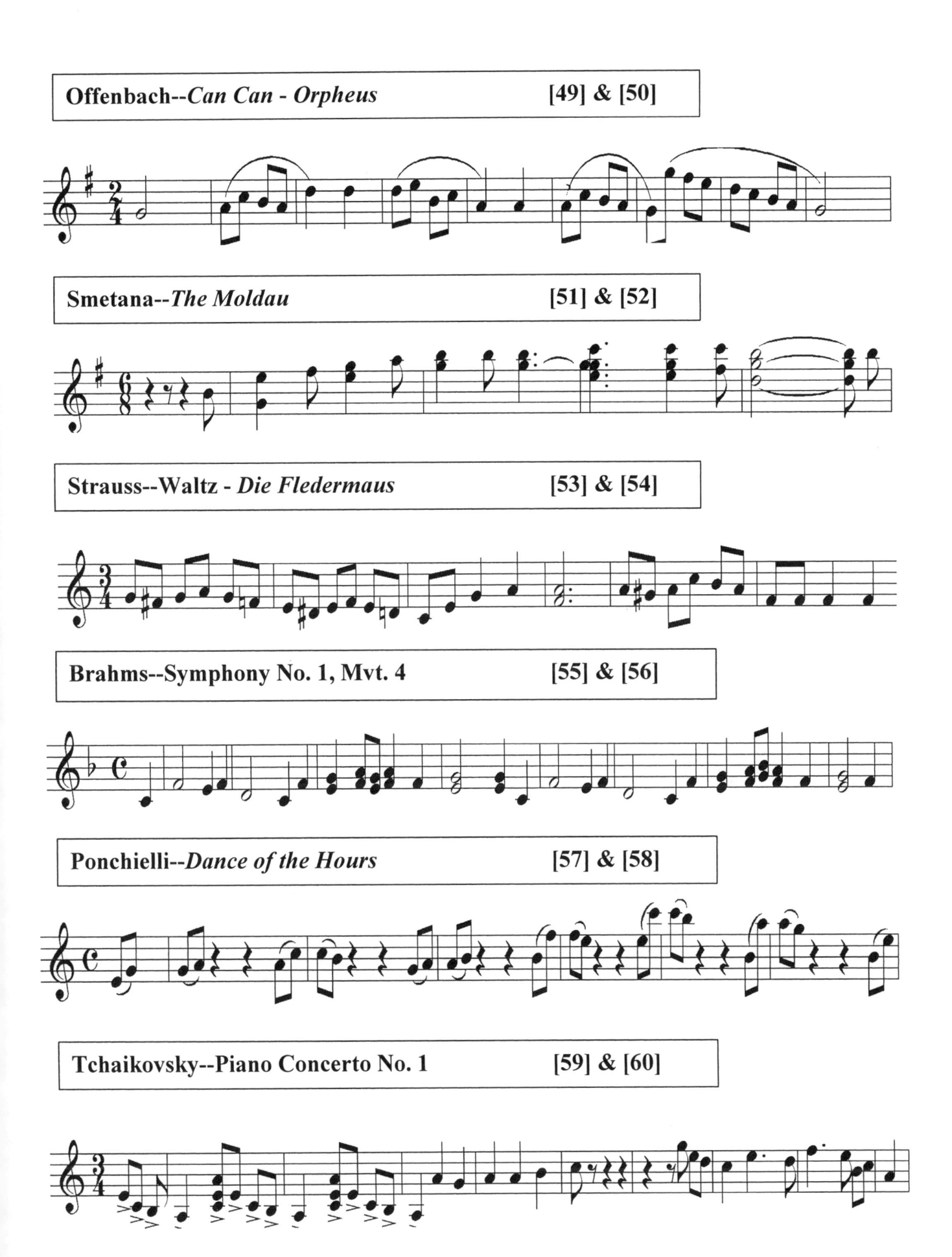

Offenbach--*Can Can - Orpheus* [49] & [50]

Smetana--*The Moldau* [51] & [52]

Strauss--Waltz - *Die Fledermaus* [53] & [54]

Brahms--Symphony No. 1, Mvt. 4 [55] & [56]

Ponchielli--*Dance of the Hours* [57] & [58]

Tchaikovsky--Piano Concerto No. 1 [59] & [60]

105

Tchaikovsky--*Sleeping Beauty* [61] & [62]

Tchaikovsky--*Romeo and Juliet* [63] & [64]

Debussy--*Reverie* [65] & [66]

Satie--*Gymnopédie* [67] & [68]

Joplin--*The Entertainer* [69] & [70]

Stravinsky--*Petrouchka* [71] & [72]

Prokofiev--*The Love for Three Oranges* [73] & [74]

APPENDIX 2---GLOSSARY

abbé - Members of the clergy not belonging to a religious order.

adagio - Slow tempo, at ease.

allegro - Fast tempo.

amateur - One who engages in an activity for pleasure rather than for money or other reasons.

aria - An elaborate melody sung by a single voice as in an opera or oratorio.

arpeggio - The notes of a chord played in order one at a time instead of together.

ballet - A theatrical performance using ballet dancing to convey a story, theme, or atmosphere.

baroque - The historical period (c.1600 - 1750) where music and art were ornate, exuberant, and dynamic.

bourrée - A French 17th century dance, or the music for that dance, in quick duple meter (two beats per measure).

band - An instrumental group composed principally of woodwind, brass, and percussion instruments.

broken chord - When each tone of a chord is played in succession instead of together.

cantata - A choral composition with choruses and solos, usually accompanied by organ, piano, or orchestra.

caricature - A cartoon likeness of a person.

chamber music - Music suited for a room or a small concert hall.

chord - A musical sound made when three or more notes are played at the same time.

coda - A concluding musical section that is formally distinct from the main structure, an added ending.

conservatory - A school specializing in one of the fine arts, such as music.

classical - Refers to music that is more complex and is more enduring than popular music.

classical magic - A magical way to remember classical music, themes, and composers.

clerical - Referring to the clergy; those who serve as ministers and priests.

compose - To create music; to write music.

concert band - Sometimes called a "symphonic band." It is larger than a pep band or a smaller town band and has more classical music in its repertory.

concerto - A composition for a full orchestra featuring a solo instrument. Usually three movements   Fast   Slow   Fast.

conduct - To lead and direct a group of musicians performing together.

da capo al fine - Italian meaning "from the beginning to the end."

107

APPENDIX 2

D. C. al Fine - (abbreviation for "da capo al fine") Go back to the beginning and play to Fine (FEE-nay), i.e. to the end, or to the finish.

dissonant - A sound that clashes, which may sound "wrong" to our ears.

étude - A study, a piece aimed at teaching a musical skill.

finale - The final part of a musical work.

fine - (FEE-nay) - The end.

forte - (FOR-tay) Loud, strong.

fugue - A "round" written for instruments.

genre - a distinctive type or category of artistic work.

grace note - An extra note played very quickly before the main note.

gavotte - A French dance in moderate 4/4 time.

homophonic - Music which has a single melody with its accompaniment.

humoresque - A humorous musical composition.

impromptu - A composition of the Romantic Period. The name implies a somewhat casual origin of the piece in the composer's mind.

improvise - To make up new music on the spot.

largo - A very slow tempo, usually combined with great expressiveness.

libretto - The words of a musical work such as an opera or an oratorio.

Mass - A musical composition which follows the form of the Roman Catholic religious service.

mazurka - A lively Polish dance in triple meter (three beats).

measure - A basic unit of musical time, usually containing two, three, or four beats.

melodious - Very pleasant to the ear, like a melody.

metronome - A mechanical or electrical device that clicks the beat at a pre-set speed to help the musician keep a steady tempo.

minuet - A slow, stately dance in triple meter (3 beats). It evolved into the waltz of the Romantic Period.

moment musical - A musical moment, a Schubert idea!

motive - Similar to a theme only much shorter.

movement - A distinct part of a musical composition, like a chapter in a book.

nocturne - A dreamy composition appropriate for nighttime.

GLOSSARY (Continued)

opera - A musical play with orchestra, chorus, solos, and people in costume who sing rather than speak their lines.

operetta - A short opera, light and sentimental, with some spoken dialogue, music, and dancing.

operaphile - one who has a great liking or attraction to opera. (See page 56.)

Opus - A work. It is used by composers and publishers to identify their works. The word is usually reserved for a collection of works of the same kind. Op. 13, No. 4 means that the music is No. 4 in Book 13. (Op. - abbreviation for Opus)

oratorio - A musical story, usually from the Bible, with soloists, chorus and orchestra, but without costumes, action or scenery. Handel's Messiah is an oratorio.

orchestra - A group of instrumentalists, especially string players, organized to play together.

orchestrate - To arrange the music for an orchestra to play.

overture - An instrumental composition meant as an introduction to an opera, oratorio, or similar work. Some overtures stand by themselves, such as *The 1812 Overture* by Tchaikovsky.

parody - To imitate a work for comic effect or ridicule.

piano - Quiet, soft.

pavane - A stately dance, or the music for this dance, from the 16th century.

piano quintet - A piano and a string quartet which has two violins, a viola and a cello.

plié - A ballet movement in which the knees are bent while the back is held straight.

polonaise - A stately Polish processional dance in triple meter.

polyphonic - Music which has two or more melodies played at the same time.

prelude - A small concert piece based on a short motive.

premiere - The first public performance.

presto - Very fast, faster than allegro.

prodigious - Extraordinary in amount, size, extent, or degree.

prodigy - A highly talented child, a really smart kid.

prolific - Producing in large quantities or with great frequency.

promenade - A leisurely walk in a public place for pleasure or display.

quartet - A musical composition for four instruments or voices. A group of four performers.

quintet - A musical composition for five instruments or voices. A group of five performers.

ragtime - Music with strong syncopation in the melody and a regularly accented accompaniment.

recitative - Music which sounds almost like speaking - used in operas and oratorios. (p.56)

APPENDIX 2

requiem - A musical setting of the Mass for the Dead.

romantic - Showing feeling, emotion.

rondo (rondeau) - A musical work or movement which has a principal theme that alternates with new themes.

scherzo - Italian word for "joke." The music is rollicking as the name suggests.

score - The copy of a musical composition in written or printed notation.

serenade - Evening music for voice or instrument.

sonata - A composition for one or two solo performers in three or four movements.

string quartet - A composition for two violins, viola and cello. Usually four movements.
Fast   Slow   Minuet   Fast.

string quintet - A composition for two violins, two violas and one cello.

suite - In general terms, a suite is a set of something, like a suite of rooms or a living room suite. In music it refers to a series of instrumental dances as in *The Nutcracker Suite*.

symphony - A composition for a full orchestra, usually four movements
Fast   Slow   Minuet   Fast.
(Symphony can also refer to the type of orchestra that plays symphonies.)

syncopated - Music in which the weak beat is accented. Jazz music uses it a lot. If you think it sounds jazzy, it's probably syncopated!

synopsis - A brief summary giving a general view of the subject.

theme - A musical idea that is developed in a composition.

toccata - A keyboard composition played (touched) very fast. Toccata comes from the Italian word *toccare* which means "to touch."

tone poem - A poem in music rather than words. Also called a symphonic poem.

trill - The quick repeating of two adjacent notes.

trio - A composition for three instruments or voices.

triple - Having three units or members.

variation - The repetition of a musical theme with modifications in rhythm, tune, harmony, or key (also called theme and variation).

vaudeville - comic theater - singing, dancing, pantomime, acrobats, comedians, (c.1880 - 1932).

vocal music - Music written for voices, either solo or chorus.

virtuoso - A performer who excels on his or her musical instrument.

waltz - A lively couple dance with three beats in a measure, evolved from the minuet.

APPENDIX 3---BIBLIOGRAPHY

Apel, Willi. *Harvard Dictionary of Music.* Cambridge: Harvard University Press, 1972.

Afanas'ev, Aleksandr. *Russian Fairy Tales.* New York: Pantheon Books, 1945.

Barlow, Harold and Morgenstern, Sam. *A Dictionary of Musical Themes.* New York: Crown, 1948.

Cross, Milton and Ewen, David. *Encyclopedia of the Great Composers and Their Music.* New York: Doubleday, 1953.

The Earl of Harewood and Peattie, Antony. *The New Kobbé's Opera Book.* New York: G.P. Putnam's Sons, 1922, 1997.

Ewen, David. *Encyclopedia of Concert Music.* New York: Hill and Wang, 1959.

Gmoser, Lulu Britz. *Great Composers.* New York: Smithmark, 1997.

Grout, Donald Jay. *The History of Western Music.* New York: W.W. Norton, 1960.

Hampton Miniature Arrow Scores, Volume 5, *The Ballets of Igor Stravinsky.*

Hoffman, E. T. A. *The Nutcracker.* Adapted by Janet Schulman. New York: Dutton, 1997.

Kamien, Roger. *Music, An Appreciation.* New York: McGraw-Hill, 1998.

Koolbergen, Jeroen. *Vivaldi.* New York: Smithmark, 1996.

Lloyd, Norman. *The Golden Encyclopedia of Music.* New York: Golden Press, 1968.

The Modern Age, The History of the World in Christian Perspective Vol. II. Pensacola: A Beka, 1981.

Pogue, David, and Speck, Scott. *Opera for Dummies.* Foster City, California: IDG Books Worldwide, 1997.

Pogue, David, and Speck, Scott. *Classical Music for Dummies.* Foster City, California: IDG Books Worldwide, 1997.

Randel, Don Michael, *Harvard Biographical Dictionary of Music,* Cambridge and London: Harvard University Press, 1996.

The Columbia Encyclopedia, Fifth Edition. New York: Houghton Mifflin, 1993.

INDEX OF CD TRACKS

TRACKS		COMPOSITION	THEME	COMPOSER	PAGE
1	2	Canon in D		Pachelbel, Johann	7
3	4	Orchestral Suite No. 1	Bourée II	Bach, Johann Sebastian	9
5	6	Minuet in G		Bach, Johann Sebastian	10
7	8	Orchestral Suite No. 1	Courante	Bach, Johann Sebastian	12
9	10	Sonata in E, K. 380		Scarlatti, Domenico	15
11	12	*The Harmonious Blacksmith*		Handel, George Frideric	17
13	14	The *Clock* Symphony	Movement 1	Haydn, Franz Joseph	25
15	16	The *Clock* Symphony	Movement 2	Haydn, Franz Joseph	27
17	18	The *Clock* Symphony	Movement 3	Haydn, Franz Joseph	32
19	20	The *Clock* Symphony	Movement 4	Haydn, Franz Joseph	33
21	22	The *Drum Roll* Symphony	Movement 4	Haydn, Franz Joseph	34
23	24	Minuet from *Don Juan*		Mozart, Amadeus	37
25	26	Piano Sonata in C - K. 545		Mozart, Amadeus	37
27	28	*Für Elise*		Beethoven, Ludwig van	39
29	30	*Turkish March*		Beethoven, Ludwig van	40
31	32	Symphony No. 5	Movement 4	Beethoven, Ludwig van	41
33	34	Serenade		Schubert, Franz	43
35	36	*Spring Song*		Mendelssohn, Felix	49
37	38	*Fantasie-Impromptu*		Chopin, Frédéric	51
39	40	*Tristesse* Etude		Chopin, Frédéric	52
41	42	*Ride of the Valkyries*		Wagner, Richard	55
43	44	*Nabucco*	Chorus of Hebrew Slaves	Verdi, Giuseppe	59
45	46	*Aïda*	*Triumphal March*	Verdi, Giuseppe	61
47	48	*Orpheus in the Underworld*	Can Can	Offenbach, Jacques	63
49	50	*Orpheus in the Underworld*		Offenbach, Jacques	65
51	52	*The Moldau*		Smetana, Bedřich	67
53	54	*Die Fledermaus*	Waltz	Strauss, Johann	69
55	56	Symphony No. 1	Movement 4	Brahms, Johannes	71
57	58	*La Gioconda*	*Dance of the Hours*	Ponchielli, Almicare	73
59	60	Piano Concerto No. 1	Movement 1	Tchaikovsky, Peter	75
61	62	*Sleeping Beauty*		Tchaikovsky, Peter	77
63	64	*Romeo and Juliet*		Tchaikovsky, Peter	79
65	66	*Reverie*		Debussy, Claude	85
67	68	*Gymnopédie*		Satie, Erik	87
69	70	*The Entertainer*		Joplin, Scott	89
71	72	*Petrouchka*		Stravinsky, Igor	93
73	74	*Love for Three Oranges*		Prokofiev, Sergei	97

INDEX OF COMPOSERS

COMPOSER	COMPOSITION	THEME	TRACKS		PAGE
Bach, Johann Sebastian	Orchestral Suite No. 1	Bourée II	3	4	9
Bach, Johann Sebastian	Minuet in G		5	6	10
Bach, Johann Sebastian	Orchestral Suite No. 1	Courante	7	8	12
Beethoven, Ludwig van	*Für Elise*		27	28	39
Beethoven, Ludwig van	*Turkish March*		29	30	40
Beethoven, Ludwig van	Symphony No. 5	Movement 4	31	32	41
Brahms, Johannes	Symphony No. 1	Movement 4	55	56	71
Chopin, Frédéric	*Fantasie-Impromptu*		37	38	51
Chopin, Frédéric	*Tristesse* Etude		39	40	52
Debussy, Claude	*Reverie*		65	66	85
Handel, George Frideric	*The Harmonious Blacksmith*		11	12	17
Haydn, Franz Joseph	The *Clock* Symphony	Movement 1	13	14	25
Haydn, Franz Joseph	The *Clock* Symphony	Movement 2	15	16	27
Haydn, Franz Joseph	The *Clock* Symphony	Movement 3	17	18	32
Haydn, Franz Joseph	The *Clock* Symphony	Movement 4	19	20	33
Haydn, Franz Joseph	The *Drum Roll* Symphony	Movement 4	21	22	34
Joplin, Scott	*The Entertainer*		69	70	89
Mendelssohn, Felix	*Spring Song*		35	36	49
Mozart, Amadeus	Minuet from *Don Juan*		23	24	37
Mozart, Amadeus	Piano Sonata in C - K. 545		25	26	37
Offenbach, Jacques	*Orpheus in the Underworld*	Can Can	47	48	63
Offenbach, Jacques	*Orpheus in the Underworld*		49	50	65
Pachelbel, Johann	Canon in D		1	2	7
Ponchielli, Almicare	*La Gioconda*	*Dance of the Hours*	57	58	73
Prokofiev, Sergei	*Love for Three Oranges*		73	74	97
Satie, Erik	*Gymnopédie*		67	68	87
Scarlatti, Domenico	Sonata in E, K. 380		9	10	15
Schubert, Franz	Serenade		33	34	43
Smetana, Bedřich	*The Moldau*		51	52	67
Strauss, Johann	*Die Fledermaus*	Waltz	53	54	69
Stravinsky, Igor	*Petrouchka*		71	72	93
Tchaikovsky, Peter	Piano Concerto No. 1	Movement 1	59	60	75
Tchaikovsky, Peter	*Sleeping Beauty*		61	62	77
Tchaikovsky, Peter	*Romeo and Juliet*		63	64	79
Verdi, Giuseppe	*Nabucco*	Chorus of Hebrew Slaves	43	44	59
Verdi, Giuseppe	*Aïda*	*Triumphal March*	45	46	61
Wagner, Richard	*Ride of the Valkyries*		41	42	55

INDEX OF COMPOSITIONS

COMPOSITION	THEME	COMPOSER	TRACKS		PAGE
Aïda	*Triumphal March*	Verdi, Giuseppe	45	46	61
Canon in D		Pachelbel, Johann	1	2	7
Die Fledermaus	Waltz	Strauss, Johann	53	54	69
Fantasie-Impromptu		Chopin, Frédéric	37	38	51
Für Elise		Beethoven, Ludwig van	27	28	39
Gymnopédie		Satie, Erik	67	68	87
La Gioconda	*Dance of the Hours*	Ponchielli, Almicare	57	58	73
Love for Three Oranges		Prokofiev, Sergei	73	74	97
Minuet from *Don Juan*		Mozart, Amadeus	23	24	37
Minuet in G		Bach, Johann Sebastian	5	6	10
Nabucco	Chorus of Hebrew Slaves	Verdi, Giuseppe	43	44	59
Orchestral Suite No. 1	Bourée II	Bach, Johann Sebastian	3	4	9
Orchestral Suite No. 1	Courante	Bach, Johann Sebastian	7	8	12
Orpheus in the Underworld	*Can Can*	Offenbach, Jacques	47	48	63
Orpheus in the Underworld		Offenbach, Jacques	49	50	65
Petrouchka		Stravinsky, Igor	71	72	93
Piano Concerto No. 1	Movement 1	Tchaikovsky, Peter	59	60	75
Piano Sonata in C - K. 545		Mozart, Amadeus	25	26	37
Reverie		Debussy, Claude	65	66	85
Ride of the Valkyries		Wagner, Richard	41	42	55
Romeo and Juliet		Tchaikovsky, Peter	63	64	79
Serenade		Schubert, Franz	33	34	43
Sleeping Beauty		Tchaikovsky, Peter	61	62	77
Sonata in E, K. 380		Scarlatti, Domenico	9	10	15
Spring Song		Mendelssohn, Felix	35	36	49
Symphony No. 1	Movement 4	Brahms, Johannes	55	56	71
Symphony No. 5	Movement 4	Beethoven, Ludwig van	31	32	41
The *Clock* Symphony	Movement 1	Haydn, Franz Joseph	13	14	25
The *Clock* Symphony	Movement 2	Haydn, Franz Joseph	15	16	27
The *Clock* Symphony	Movement 3	Haydn, Franz Joseph	17	18	32
The *Clock* Symphony	Movement 4	Haydn, Franz Joseph	19	20	33
The *Drum Roll* Symphony	Movement 4	Haydn, Franz Joseph	21	22	34
The Entertainer		Joplin, Scott	69	70	89
The Harmonious Blacksmith		Handel, George Frideric	11	12	17
The Moldau		Smetana, Bedřich	51	52	67
Tristesse Etude		Chopin, Frédéric	39	40	52
Turkish March		Beethoven, Ludwig van	29	30	40